THE WISDOM YEARS

A Spirituality of Aging
Reflection and Ripening, Harvest and Homecoming

MARGARET SILF

Paulist Press
New York / Mahwah, NJ

First published in 2025 by Darton, Longman and Todd Ltd in the United Kingdom. editorial@darton-longman-todd.co.uk

ISBN: 978-0-8091-5807-2 (paperback)

Library of Congress Control Number: 2025941309

This edition published by
Paulist Press
997 Macarthur Boulevard
Mahwah, NJ 07430
www.paulistpress.com

Printed and bound in India by Replika Press Pvt. Ltd.

CONTENTS

Prologue 5

Chapter 1: Welcome to Wisdom Country 9
Chapter 2: Amber Lights 27
Chapter 3: Letting Go 42
Chapter 4: Winter Gifts 57
Chapter 5: Independence? 73
Chapter 6: Coming Down the Mountain 89
Chapter 7: The Bigger Picture 103
Chapter 8: When the Seed Dies 119
Chapter 9: Our Legacy to the Future 136

Epilogue 155
Acknowledgements 158

PROLOGUE

'The real voyage of discovery consists not in seeking new landscapes but in having new eyes.'
Marcel Proust

AS WE EMBARK on this voyage of discovery through our later years, we are not looking for new landscapes. Most of us already know the landscape of older age all too well, and not all of it is easy or comfortable. But do we need new eyes?

How we see the landscape of aging depends very much on the culture that has shaped us. Ancient, mainly eastern wisdom, as well as our own experience, suggests that life tends to reveal a pattern of four stages. The first quarter of life is the time of learning, as children and young adults. In the second quarter, traditionally seen as the 'householder and parenting' stage, we establish homes and families and embark on our working lives. The third quarter is the season of consolidating our careers as we approach retirement and children fly the nest. The fourth quarter is, especially in Hindu philosophy, the season of renunciation, a time to withdraw 'to the forest' and reflect more deeply on spiritual things. We who now find ourselves in these 'forest years' will also be engaged in reflecting back over our lives and their meaning and facing the challenges of letting go.

Of course these stages are not to be taken rigidly, but if we think about them I wonder how we would view them. If we have been shaped by Western culture, we will have been conditioned by social norms to regard the second and third stages as the most important, these being the seasons of productivity, keeping the world turning and the economy going so that enough wealth is generated to support those in the first and fourth stages. Children and older people tend to be seen as marginal to this central engine of life, either not yet or no longer 'productive'.

This might be the view you would see through the 'old eyes'.

How might this appear if we had 'new eyes'?

Seen through a different lens, we might focus primarily on the first and the fourth stages as the seasons of spiritual growth and awareness. The child is unconsciously absorbing countless new experiences daily and processing them into the miracle we call 'mind'. The elder, or forest dweller, is looking back over a life of experience and distilling it, through reflection, into wisdom. These are crucial stages of spiritual development for humanity as a whole, if we are to evolve to higher levels of consciousness and become the best human beings we can be. The second and third stages could be regarded as maintenance seasons, keeping the world turning and in good shape. This is in no way to detract from the importance of these maintenance seasons. Without them we could not exist, in material terms, on the planet. However, as we intuit in our own hearts and are reminded in Christian scripture, 'humankind does not live from bread alone'.

'New eyes' reveal the deep spiritual significance of the shoulder seasons of youth and age, during which we are more engaged with human *being*, than with human *doing.* The journey that lies ahead in the pages of this book takes a fresh look at the fourth season, the wisdom years, from this radically changed perspective. However, you don't really need new eyes. The eyes of your soul are already there and awakened. All they need is some re-focusing in order to see the signposts along the path of older age for what they really are – pointers and invitations to discover the immense spiritual value of our later years and to recognise, harvest and share the fruits of a life well lived.

CHAPTER 1

WELCOME TO WISDOM COUNTRY

Wisdom is not a station you arrive at
but a manner of travelling.
Sue Monk Kidd

IF YOU HAVE ever spent time exploring outback Australia you may have had the experience of being greeted by the indigenous custodians of a particular region with their *Welcome to Country*, a formal ceremony of welcome performed by a tribal elder. In turn, most public events in Australia begin with an *Acknowledgement of Country* which recognises the traditional custodians of the land on which the event is happening and pays respect to the elders, past, present and to come. The event or gathering thus becomes part of a much longer story, firmly placed in a wider context and grounded in a spirit of gratitude and humility.

This book is, in its own small way, an acknowledgement of the long story of wisdom's unfolding through the generations and a welcome to this vast and sacred landscape that we might call Wisdom Country. Aging is a portal into this country and an invitation to discover your later years as wisdom years, with the potential to bear rich fruit not only for yourself, but for all creation.

In spite of this personal welcome to a country where wisdom dwells, the possibility of dwelling there yourself may have surprised you. Is it perhaps a little pretentious to claim that our later years might also be our 'wisdom years'? is it just wishful thinking? What makes us think that simply being older would make us wiser?

Well let's start right there. We have not just grown older, we have lived longer. We are in our senior years in the University of Life. But simply living longer doesn't automatically bestow wisdom. It merely provides experience.

So what is wisdom anyway? How does it happen? Does it come from education? A friend of mine, who had never had the chance of higher education, once raised a few eyebrows in a gathering by coming out with a very wise comment on a particular situation. Afterwards someone expressed surprise at these wise words from someone so lacking in formal education. This was a lightbulb moment for me. It was suddenly clear that wisdom doesn't come from education, but from *experience*.

Education gives us knowledge. Experience gives us wisdom ... *but only if we reflect on it.*

The Greek philosopher Socrates is reputed to have said that 'an unexamined life is not worth living'. What might this mean for us, and how do we do this reflecting? Gaining in age doesn't necessarily lead to wisdom, and the old adage warns us that 'there is no fool like an old fool'. Wisdom doesn't come in a package delivered on our seventieth birthday. It is the fruit of a reflective life. So how might our own lives bear the fruit of this elusive gift?

Our later years bring us many challenges as we already know. But they also bring a gift we may not have enjoyed much in our youth – the gift of time. Time to think back over our lives – over what is most important to us now and what is less so – time for regrets and time for gratitude – time to notice the shape our lives have taken and how we feel about it.

They also bring the gift of perspective. The longer we have lived, the more experiences we have garnered and the more we can begin to see how things hang together. We start to recognise what seems off-key in our life, and what resonates with our deepest self. We learn to distinguish between what is, and has remained, truly important to us, and what only seemed important at the time. We see more clearly what is truly reflecting our own hearts and souls and what we have just taken on board from those around us, from our culture or from the expectations of our society.

These gifts that come with our later years are an invitation to grow into fruitful spiritual maturity if we have the courage to embrace and use them. We know that the quality of a wine increases with age. The grapes from the late harvest are valued more highly than those gathered earlier in the season, and the finest wines are made from the grapes harvested after the first frosts. This is encouraging. It tells us two things: first, age brings something special to the party, and second, that special quality often comes after a period of hardship – our personal frosty seasons when we may feel life is dealing us a tough hand. So yes, not just a time to be settling down with pipe and slippers and a rocking chair but also the time for serious soul work, for which we were not ready in our earlier years.

The world-renowned French cognac grapes grow only in the region of Cognac, after which they are named. If you ask the local vintners why this is, and what special qualities this region possesses, they will tell you that two factors give these grapes their unique flavour: first, the clarity of light in that area, and second, the stony ground on which the vines grow, which forces their roots to become stronger as they establish themselves in the soil. Age brings a certain clarity to the elders of society too, if they have reflected on their long experience, and the 'stony ground' is also apparent as old age approaches and life becomes, in many ways, tougher and more challenging.

We may even find that our frailty is itself a powerful catalyst for new discovery, as the following little story suggests…

There was once an ancient community who were the guardians of a precious golden figure of the Buddha. This figure was very important to the community and they cherished it. But one day there came rumours of war along their borders. A hostile army was on the march.

The people were very anxious to protect their precious golden Buddha from the advancing troops, who would surely take it as loot. And so they covered the statue in mud so that its beauty and value would not attract unwanted attention, and then they hid it in a ditch covered in tangled undergrowth, quite out of sight.

The years passed, the invading army came and

went, the war was over and the golden Buddha was forgotten, even by the members of the community. One day a passer-by was walking along a country lane and happened to notice a glint of something shining through the weeds and brambles. Closer examination revealed a cracked and grimy mud-covered statue with hints of gold showing through in parts. The precious golden Buddha had been re-discovered, almost forgotten, but now being naturally restored to its full beauty as the dried mud cracked and fell away. The treasure was back home, cherished again in the heart of the community.

There is a uniquely precious centre in each of us, but life can sometimes be very hostile, and other people can threaten or hurt us, so we conceal our true selves behind masks, cover them with mud and bury them in hidden places to protect our vulnerable centre.

And then comes older age. The mud begins to crack, the masks start falling off. Gleams of the authentic golden centre are sometimes glimpsed, if not by ourselves, then by those around us. The crumbling of our defences may be the very thing that reveals our gold to the world.

How does this story speak to *you*?

REFLECTIVE LIVING

It's easy to talk about the need to reflect on our experience, but how do you actually do this?

Practising reflective living is a bit like reading a compass when you are out on a hike. This requires three things:

- A map of the terrain you are exploring
- The ability to read the compass
- Time to stand still while you take the reading.

How does this translate into the skill of reflecting on the events of everyday life?

In Christian spirituality we find a host of examples, just by watching Jesus of Nazareth at work.

He typically begins by inviting people to think about how they spend their time, or earn their living – looking after sheep, ploughing the fields, tending their gardens, sweeping their homes, baking their bread. In other words, he is asking them to look at the map of the terrain of their everyday lives.

Now that he has attracted their attention, they are standing still and listening. They are taking the time to think about what they are hearing. They have stopped what they were doing for a short time, and they are going to learn something – something that will connect their own lives with the vast universe of the Holy.

He then goes on to show them how to read the compass, how to make the crucial connections that will lead them to a deeper level of wisdom. For example, he shares the secret that the tiniest seed they plant in their fields and gardens has the potential to grow into a tree big enough for birds to build a nest in, or that it takes only a few grains of yeast to turn a whole bowl of flour into bread to feed the family. What might this mean to the discouraged gardener surveying a winter-stricken patch of earth or an overburdened mother wondering what difference her small contribution to the world could possibly make? What might it mean to you?

WELCOME TO WISDOM COUNTRY

An approach to the art of reflective living …

- Step back and take a look at the terrain of your daily life. This is where the seeds of wisdom dwell.
- Carve out some time to be still, to make time and space for the wisdom seeds in your own experience to germinate and grow.
- During this time of stillness, notice what is going on in your life and what these things mean to you.

WISDOM'S HIDING PLACES

Your life is a goldmine of wisdom if you know where to look. Wisdom plants its seeds in many places. Perhaps some of these examples reflect your own experience?

- People who have guided you – wisdom figures in your life
- Significant experiences of loss or grief
- Significant experiences of joy
- Music, art or literature that has taken you to deeper reaches of yourself
- Your work and/or any colleagues or mentors in that context
- Your religious or spiritual tradition
- Your deepest desires
- Any significant or recurring dreams
- Key personal relationships in your life
- Fears, disappointments or failures and how you overcame them
- The wisdom of the natural world, the creatures who share it with us, the skies above us and the earth beneath our feet.

Have you found wisdom in any of these sources? Any other sources?

Be specific in your memories. What particular wisdom have you gained?

COLLECTIVE WISDOM

Wisdom, we could say, is woven into the fabric of the universe. There is a deep well of wisdom from which we can draw, of which our own personal wisdom is merely a small droplet We only need to reflect on the origins of our universe to discover the amazing story of our beginnings and the intricate and beautiful web of relationship with all creation, to which we belong and in which every sub-atomic particle is connected to every other.

Barbara Brown Taylor (in *The Luminous Web*) vividly reminds us that

> *It took all the chemistry*
> *Since Big Bang*
> *To pedigree*
> *The DNA union*
> *That is 'me'.*

We know, if we are honest, that we all stand on giants' shoulders, but this truth came home to me especially forcefully one day when I was in the garden of St Antony's Priory in Durham, about to begin a day of reflection and feeling very aware of the inadequacy of anything I could offer to the people who would be attending. The view from that garden was spectacular, its main focus being the majestic Durham Cathedral. It was suddenly very obvious that everything we know in our twenty-first century lives has come down to us from all those who have gone before, seeking tirelessly after truth, and that our task is to build on that legacy and add the fragment of our own discoveries to the collective wisdom of humankind.

We are part of a long continuum of human life and discovery, successors to those who built that cathedral stone by stone, those who lie buried in its precincts and those whose prayer has soaked into its walls through the centuries. We walk our own life-paths in the footsteps of all our ancestors and we do well to recall that it is, first and foremost, the indigenous peoples of the world, of America, Africa, Asia and Australia and of our Celtic northern isles, who have the most to teach us about wisdom. These are the giants from whose broad shoulders we can see, for example:

- That we belong to a great web of life, and what we do to the web we do to ourselves
- That wisdom is not an individual attainment but a cumulative gift to be received from those who have gone before us and passed on to those who follow after
- That the land does not belong to us but we belong to the land
- That we have a responsibility to make all our decisions keeping in mind the effects of our choices on 'the seventh generation', meaning all who follow after us
- That we have the most to learn from the elders among us, who have lived the longest and who are to be cherished, and not carelessly consigned to 'history'.

If you are in any doubt about your own access to wisdom, reflect on this long and sacred narrative and your own unique part in it, and on the course your own life has taken. You are standing in the heart of a goldmine.

A LIFE REMEMBERED

On my fiftieth birthday I took a detour on the way back from town one morning. I drove to our local university campus at Keele and went on a nostalgia walk. That place had witnessed a great deal of my story since I was a graduate student there. My spiritual story was very significantly shaped by people and events there. Some good, amazing even. Others challenging and painful.

Eventually I found my way to an ancient oak tree standing proud on the campus lawns. Its roots were surrounded by a circle of freshly emerging crocuses, heralds of spring, and my heart took flight.

As I stood there, reflecting over all that had happened through the years, I knew that everything that had transpired in my life – the good, the bad and the ugly – had brought me to this day, this place, this moment. And this was a good place, a good moment that would not have been, but for all that went before and would be the beginning of everything still to come.

Ignatian spirituality suggests the practice of a daily reflection (sometimes called the Examen) on what the day has brought. For what are we grateful? What, if anything, do we regret? What has made us feel more alive and why? What has left us feeling a bit flat, or even angry, and why?

Whether or not this has been part of your practice, now might be the time to do a Life Reflection, or Life Examen. This could include reflecting on things like:

- What in your life, has brought you real joy? For what are you especially grateful?
- What has caused you pain or regret?
- Which people or events have most profoundly shaped your life
- Are any thank you letters due? Or any apologies?
- What experiences have taught you the most?
- When your life is ebbing away how might you feel – what might you wish you had spent more time and energy on – more time with family and friends, for example?
- How would you like to be remembered?

Take some time to think about how you might approach this task. Begin by letting memories rise to consciousness spontaneously and noticing what is striking you. Then go back to what seems most important and reflect on it more deeply, seeking to recognise what Wisdom is offering you.

There are many ways of doing this, perhaps in writing, perhaps in visual form, and there are several powerful images that might help you. For example:

Imagining your life as a river, noticing where the flow has been calm and steady, and where it has hit the rapids. Where did your river begin and where is its destination? What obstacles and detours has it encountered? What or who has added to your river's flow, and what fruits has it borne?

Imagining your life as a pathway or a mountain climb. What joyful surprises has it revealed, and where has it been hard-going? Which companions have travelled with you along your path? What sustained you along the path and what obstacles did you encounter?

Imagining your life as a journey, perhaps by train or bus. What route did the journey take? What unexpected changes did it make? What diversions or accidents did it encounter? What kind of landscape has it passed through? Who came on board as fellow passengers along the way and who disembarked when their own journey was finished? Where are you now along the route? How do you view the destination?

Reflecting on the deepest dreams, desires and ambitions that have shaped your journey. How have they been fulfilled, quite probably not in the ways you might have imagined when you were younger.

You might even imagine your life journey in the shape of a tree - a wisdom tree. Which branches have been most important to you? Which deep roots most nourish your tree (for example, family, friends, landscape, cultural heritage)? What has helped your tree to grow? Remember both the joy and warmth of the sunshine times, the refreshing (or annoying) rainfall, the storms and the hard frosts – they have all shaped your journey.

PAYING ATTENTION TO THE SCARS AND MIS-STEPS

As you reflect back over your life path, it's worth asking yourself what kind of experience has taught you the most? Your achievements or your failures? Your strengths or your weaknesses? Your triumphs or your blunders? The good times or the bad? Your medals or your scars?

Wisdom often grows better among the weeds of our lives than in our carefully cultivated flower beds. Every teacher, parent or carer will know that the most powerful learning points in children's lives (and indeed in the lives of adults too) happen when there is a red cross against the homework or a reprimand regarding a mistake. At these moments we have to stop and think, and be open to correction and guidance. They are like awkward stiles along a country walk. Your progress is temporarily impeded and you have to make an effort to climb over the stile. The stile may seem like an unwelcome obstruction, but in fact it is the gateway to a whole new field of understanding.

Perhaps the wisest person is the one who has made the most mistakes and learned from them.

I am always reminded of this when I stand beneath a starry sky and trace the pattern of the constellation of The Plough. If you find and follow the last two stars of The Plough, they will point to the North Star, which provides an apparently fixed point in the heavens to aid navigation. When you turn towards the North Star you are facing true north.

Yet if you could draw a line along the stars in this constellation it would be a very crooked line indeed, like a dog's hind leg. If you followed it you would, at certain points along your journey, be travelling south rather than north. Often when I've been feeling confused or dispirited by my own apparent failures and wrong choices, The Plough (also known as the Big Dipper or Great Bear) has gently reassured me that however disjointed and directionless my life may at times have been, it has also, at some deep level, been reliably nudging me towards my own inner 'true north', where I am living true to my own best values.

A DIFFERENT KIND OF LIFE STORY

... About trusting the journey into transformation.

Once, a long time ago, a little tree was growing in the forest. As the little tree grew taller and stronger, she began to notice the wide expanse of sky stretching far above her head. She noticed the white clouds scudding across the sky, as if on some great journey. She watched the birds wheeling overhead and flying beyond the horizon.

The skies, the clouds, the birds in flight – they all seemed to speak of a land beyond the horizon, a land of forever. The more she grew, the more she noticed these forever things, and the more she longed to live forever herself.

One day the forester happened to pass close by the little tree. He was a kindly man, and he sensed that the little tree was not entirely happy. 'What's the matter, little tree?' he asked. 'What troubles your soul?'

The little tree hesitated, and then told the forester about her secret dream: 'I would so much like to live forever.'

'Perhaps you shall,' replied the forester. 'Perhaps you shall.'

Some time passed, and once again the forester passed close by the little tree, now grown tall and strong.

'Do you still want to live forever?' he asked the tree.

'Oh I do, I do,' the tree replied fervently.

'I think I can help, but first you must give me your permission to cut you down.'

The tree was aghast: 'I wanted to live forever. And now you say you are going to kill me?'

'I know,' said the forester. 'It sounds crazy. But if you can trust me, I promise you that your secret dream will be fulfilled.'

After much hard thought, the tree gave her consent. The forester came with his sharp-bladed axe. The tree was felled. The sap of life streamed away and was lost in the forest floor. The tender wood was sliced into strips. The strips were planed and shaped and smothered in a suffocating layer of varnish. The tree screamed silently in her anguish, but there was no way back. She surrendered herself to the hands of the violin-

maker, and all dreams of foreverness vanished in a haze of pain.

For many years the violin lay idle. Sometimes she remembered better days, when she was growing in the woods. What a bad bargain it had been, surrendering herself to the forester's axe. How could she have been so naïve as to believe that this would enable her to live forever?

But the day came – the right and perfect moment – when the violin was gently lifted from her case and caressed once more by loving hands. She held her breath in disbelief. She quivered as the bow tenderly crossed her breast. And the quivering turned into a pure sound that reminded her of how the wind had once rustled through her leaves, how the clouds had once scudded by on their way to forever, how the birds had wheeled overhead, shaping circles of eternity in the blue sky.

A pure sound. Pure notes. The music of Forever.

'My wood has turned to music!' the tree gasped deep inside herself. The forester spoke the truth.'

And the music resounded, from listening heart to listening heart, down through all the ages until, at last, when all the listening hearts had made their own journey home, it rolled through the gates of eternity, where the little tree became a Forever Tree.

PAUSE FOR THOUGHT

- What has struck you most in this introduction to 'the wisdom years'? Perhaps something has especially resonated, or maybe something has irritated you or made you feel uncomfortable. Notice any strong reactions, either positive or negative, as these are indicators of points asking for your further attention.
- Do you already have a spiritual practice to help you find inner stillness and a space where reflection can lead to wisdom? If not, do you feel drawn to any of the suggestions in this chapter?
- When you reflect back over your life, where, in hindsight, do you feel you have found sources of wisdom?
- How do you feel about the mistakes and apparent failures in your life? Might these be important points of growth in your journey to wisdom? How

might this shape your attitude to the faults and failures of others?

- You might like to spend some quality time now in composing your own life review. This could give you a helpful map of your journey towards the wisdom years, and would be a useful introduction to the journey we will be making in the remainder of this book.
- How do you feel about the story of the Forever Tree? Can you believe that even those times in your life that seemed destructive have been helping to bring your best and truest self to birth? This is one of the great gifts of the longer perspective that the years bestow.

CHAPTER 2

AMBER LIGHTS

We cannot live the afternoon of life according to the programme of life's morning.
C. G. Jung

A COLLEAGUE OF mine worked shifts as a computer operator, back in the days when a computer occupied a hall as big as a warehouse and needed a team of operators to look after it night and day, responding to its various cries for help, and keeping it fed with data on punched cards. It was two o'clock in the morning. He had just finished a busy late night shift and the demands of his charge had left him exhausted. He drove along the country lanes on his way home, but when he had to stop at a set of traffic lights, he fell fast asleep. We never knew how long his nap lasted, certainly through several cycles of the lights, but it came to an abrupt end at the sound of a sharp tap on his car window. As he wound down the window a puzzled police officer enquired, most politely: 'Don't you like *any* of our colours, sir?'

Amber Lights are a signal to slow down and prepare to stop. Whether we like it or not, we will (possibly sooner than we think) STOP. For now we are in the process of slowing down, and this has the unexpected benefit of giving us the opportunity to do the essential reflecting on our experience that turns it into wisdom.

Wisdom grows when we reflect on our experience, but reflection requires time, intentional focus, and above all – *stillness.* Just as in the natural world we only see those beautiful reflections in the lake or river when the waters are completely still, so our own reflection needs an inner stillness that often eludes us. Our later years certainly offer us the invitation to slow down and stand still, whether willingly or not. They invite us to let go of the frenzied busy-ness of our former working lives, to allow time to calm the turbulence that in hindsight seems to have served no useful purpose. (Remember all those meetings that so often decided nothing more than the date of the next meeting?). And then – and here's the problem – they remind us not to fill our lives up again with a new set of needless busy-ness.

We all heard the call to stand still in 2020 when the COVID-19 pandemic literally brought the world to a standstill. During those months of lockdown and severely restricted movement there was something deeply restorative in the absence of speeding traffic or aircraft flying overhead, or the busy schedules that normally crowd our diaries. Without a doubt this time brought severe hardship, and tragic loss in its wake, but it does no harm to remember that it was also a call to slow down and reflect on what really mattered most in our lives and cultivate wiser attitudes towards the ways we spend our time.

Some years ago I had a conversation with a young man recently divorced, who had lost his home and former lifestyle, and had only limited contact with his children. He had plenty of regrets, but I was very moved when he told me that the whole experience had stopped him in his tracks and made him think more deeply about what mattered most to him. 'I used to think it was all about having a fast car, a nice house and two good holidays a year,' he told me. 'Now I realise that only two things matter: how I spend my time and who with.' In his very painful experience, this young man had discovered that life and relationships were far more important to him than anything money could buy. So you don't have to be old to be wise – but it helps.

We can't change the fact that life is inevitably calling us to slow down. What we *can* change is our *attitude* to the situation in which we find ourselves.

Are you perhaps feeling regret, or even resentment, that you can no longer do the things you used to enjoy doing, or ever again visit the places and people you have loved? Or is it gratitude that you ever had these blessings, and now have the memories. Probably it's a mixture of these responses, but what matters is where we mainly choose to focus our energy – on the regrets or the gratitude.

Whenever the regrets take over, I try quite consciously to turn them round. For example: 'I regret that I will never travel to my favourite country again' can be turned into 'I'm so grateful that I ever had the chance to travel there at all'. You may find that the feelings of gratitude turn out to be much stronger and more life-giving than the feelings of regret that they have replaced.

Every experience in your life has the potential to change you. You have been shaped and formed by all that life has given you – and indeed by all that life has taken away from you.

Which of these phrases speaks more to you: 'I wish I had…', or 'I'm glad I did'?

- Do you know anyone who exemplifies the attitude of gratitude?
- Or anyone who seems to live in a world of regret?
- What do you learn from these people?

A traditional African tale has much to teach us about gratitude…

Once upon a time a traveller was walking in the bush when, out of sheer malice, a monkey sitting on a high tree branch threw a coconut at him.

The man rubbed his bruised head, and then stooped to pick up the coconut. First he drank the milk. Then he ate the tender flesh of the coconut. And then he sat down in a shady spot and patiently carved a bowl out of the coconut shell.

And finally he looked up to the treetop and thanked the monkey and went on his way.

DIMINISHMENT

As we age, we (at least in our western culture) often feel that we are side-lined by the wider population, bereft of any status we may once have had, no longer respected as productive members of society, just a burden on the health and social services. The young might see us as relics from a former age, though they probably wouldn't say this to our face.

This is not a comfortable process – because what is actually happening is the shrinking of our EGO.

Which makes it extremely important. An oversized ego makes it impossible to go through the proverbial narrow gate. All spiritual traditions seem to agree that, while we need to build up our ego in the first half of life (to keep the world turning, recognise and develop our skills, further our careers and establish the necessary boundary between 'myself' and 'other'), the task of the second half of life is to let our ego shrink, and move to a deeper plane of being, where 'me' and 'my' become less central and 'myself' gradually becomes more closely interwoven with the wider reality of all creation.

In our later years we may also discover that 'less is more'. In general we are not so interested in accumulating material things but rather in shedding them. When asked what we want for a birthday or Christmas gift, we may well choose to spend quality time with those we love rather than any material gift. The long Santa lists of childhood have been distilled down to their essential spirit and the deep truth comes home to us, that the greater blessing really does lie in giving and sharing than in receiving and acquiring.

The children's game of Pass-the-Parcel can help us understand how this works. The parcel, containing the prize wrapped in layers and layers of packaging, is passed around from child to child while music is played. When the music stops, the child holding the parcel can begin, or continue, unwrapping it, until the music starts again, when the parcel has to be passed on. When the music stops for the last time the child with the parcel gets the prize.

This game is a metaphor for life, especially as

we face the slowdown and diminishment of age. The prize, our true self, stripped of all non-essentials, is wrapped in thick layers of the things we thought were so important when we were younger. The music stops in many different ways: through illness or injury, through the loss of job or status, through bereavement or the loss of a valued relationship. Whenever the music stops (in our lives) we come a little closer to the treasure at the centre. Another layer of the 'more' is stripped away and we are taken, perhaps reluctantly and probably painfully, a little closer to the 'pearl of great price'. When the music stops for the last time, logically we should find the treasure.

I once had the experience of guiding an individually-given retreat in a beautiful area in Wales. It was Maytime and the natural world was in full bloom – blossom and fresh green growth all around, and, unusually, the weather was wonderful too. Ideal conditions for a perfect retreat. I was very happy for the retreatants, who would be able to explore the surrounding countryside and bask in the spring sunshine.

But that's not how it turned out. The retreat centre itself was situated in extensive grounds, with an orchard, woodland and several paths leading out into the surrounding hills and lanes. So it was with some dismay that we discovered a notice nailed to every gate leading to the outside world, forbidding access. The reason? An outbreak of foot and mouth disease in the local area, meaning that every affected farm was in quarantine, and all public access restricted, for the protection of the animals.

At first I felt regret for the retreatants but my regret was soon challenged by one of the people I was accompanying. He began the week by sharing with me his joy in exploring the retreat centre grounds and all he was discovering. Gradually over the following days his focus narrowed, first down to the confines of just the orchard, and eventually settling on a single tree stump. I listened, spell-bound, as he told me all the ways in which that tree stump, with its own amazing miniature ecosystem, had drawn his heart and mind more deeply into the holiness of creation. He was discovering more and more in less and less. By the end of the retreat it seemed he had found almost everything in almost nothing.

As we age we may find ourselves restricted in our movements, or confined to a small space in our own homes or elsewhere. Of course this can feel depressing, but perhaps the wisdom of the (adapted) saying could help: 'If you can't be in the place you love, love the place you're in.' In younger years we can be so occupied in the big wide world that we can miss the beauty that is on our own doorstep. The restrictions of age require us to adjust our focus to close range. A friend of mine, living with her family in a cramped apartment in an urban area wanted to incorporate a period of stillness into her daily routine, but had no space to make a special corner. As she reviewed her living space, she noticed a tree growing close to her window in the communal back yard and she decided to take it as her focus for her quiet reflection time. The tree became a cherished companion, changing day by day through every season and never failing to draw her into the deeper stillness she was seeking.

I was once forced into an unwanted slowdown which became the gateway to unexpected treasure. I was in a hurry to get a parcel to the post office in the nearby village, and equally in a hurry to get back home again. However, in the post office I met an elderly neighbour whom I knew only by sight. We left the post office together and it was obvious that we were both heading in the same homeward direction. It would have been impossibly discourteous for me not to have walked back home, up a steep hill, with him, but this meant taking a very slow pace, as he was not very mobile and had to keep stopping for a rest. There was nothing I could do about it, but walk alongside him and make the best of the unexpected delay to my busy schedule. And as we walked he told me something of his story – what he had done in his life, where he had lived, what things had inspired him. It was an engrossing experience, and it made me realise how much I was missing by not really getting to know my neighbours. But it took the amber lights to slow me down sufficiently to listen.

LIVING IN THE AMBER LIGHTS ZONE

The amber lights are a call to come to stillness. Your life may have moved from active engagement with the working world to different kinds of activity, such as more time with friends and family, volunteering in various ways, or taking up new hobbies and activities.

The stillness challenge isn't about passive inactivity but about finding stillness in the deeper reaches of our being. It's there that we will find the space to reflect on what matters most in our lives.

This may happen in many different ways, for example

- Familiar meditative or mindfulness practices
- Listening, with focused attention, to family, friends, the world around us.
- Reflective walking, being present to the natural world in slower, deeper ways
- Creative practices such as music-making, painting or photography, that help us to be present to the present moment and give it our full attention.

When life is troubled and you can't see the way ahead, it can help to imagine yourself holding a glass of muddy water, straight from a murky river. It takes time for the water to settle, but with the passing of time you would find that the mud settles at the bottom of the glass and the water becomes clear. The time it takes for this to happen in our lives is 'amber lights time'.

As we age, we become better able to allow time for life to settle again after the inevitable storms. We are less inclined to rush into hasty 'fixes' or half-baked solutions. We have learned that the breakthrough moments often come when we stop straining for them. In stillness life has a chance to open up for us the way ahead. Some would say this is divine guidance at work. Others might call it the gentle (or sometimes not-so-gentle) promptings of the universe.

A well-known hymn expresses it like this:

Drop thy still dews of quietness
Till all our strivings cease;
Take from our souls the strain and stress,
And let our ordered lives confess
The beauty of thy peace.

(John Greenleaf Whittier)

Whatever we call it, stillness is the key to letting our inner wisdom speak to us 'through the strain and stress' and shape our next move.

What helps *you* to come to this inner stillness?

ACTION AND CONTEMPLATION: A WINNING TEAM

Perhaps you have experienced the tension that can arise between those who are activists, always on the front line of protests and demonstrations in pursuit of peace and justice, and those who hold back from the front line and feel drawn to engage with the big questions of humanity in the quiet space of their own hearts. Does it have to be 'either-or'? There are many roads – both highways and by-ways – on the journey towards wisdom.

I was reminded of this when I was given an oil lamp by a good friend. Whenever I lit it, it told me a story about life. Its whole function depended on the wick

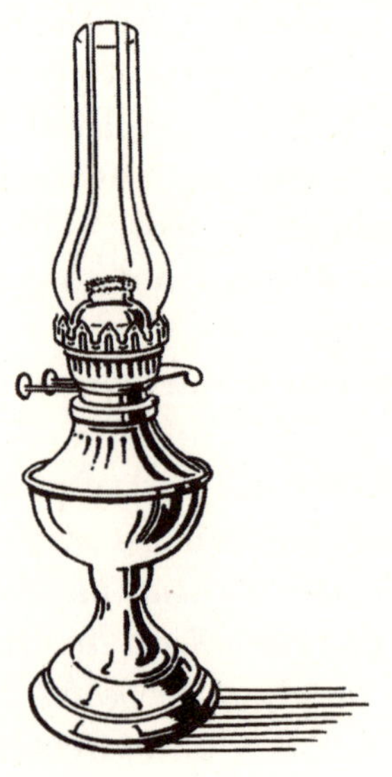

and the wick had two ends. One end was immersed in the oil and the other extended out into the world. Both of those conditions needed to be in place if there was to be a flame. If the wick was not immersed in the oil there would be no fuel for the flame and if it was not extended into the world, its potential for light and warmth would never be realised.

As we reflect on the need for stillness to allow the growth of wisdom, this delicate relationship between contemplation and action, between the oil and the flame, comes into new focus. Whether you see yourself as mainly a contemplative or mainly an activist, remember that the wick has two ends, both equally necessary if there is to be light. We don't have to be both ends ourselves. We just need to understand that we complement each other and are both equally needed in the journey of life.

A little story honours this relationship:

The Human Qualities Olympic Games were underway and there was great excitement around the track events. The two favourites were Enthusiasm and Steadfastness. Enthusiasm took off at great speed and was soon way ahead, with Steadfastness lagging behind. But halfway through Enthusiasm started to flag and Steadfastness gradually closed in, until eventually Steadfastness crossed the finishing line and won the Gold.

Once the excitement had died down, Enthusiasm and Steadfastness shook hands. 'You always get things going,' said Steadfastness to Enthusiasm. 'I really admire your energy.' 'But I never make the distance on my own,' replied Enthusiasm. 'It's you who bring things to completion.' From then on the two always ran together as a team, never seeing each other as competitors, but as collaborators in the race of life.

One of the challenges of the wisdom years is the gradual move from 'either/or' to 'both/and'. We are no longer at home in a dualistic world with its constant demands to choose between 'good' and 'bad', and we begin to inhabit a world that embraces all our differences, recognising the unique value of each person and the merits in all sides of any question.

BEFRIENDING IMPERFECTION

The passing of the years teaches us more and more forcefully that life is far from perfect. Our need to get everything right gives way to a different attitude to such perfectionism.

How comfortable do you feel with imperfection, in life and in yourself? Try checking out your responses to these suggestions:

- The dinner doesn't have to be on the table at 6pm sharp.
- The housework can wait because it's more important to be with a friend.
- The clothes I bought ten years ago are still perfectly fine.
- Mis-shaped veggies taste as good as those that are 'perfectly formed'.
- I don't have anything to prove. My friends love me just as I am.

Do you notice any 'imperfections' in your own life that you are now better able to accept? Any that you still find difficult?

There is a tendency for people who strive for perfection in their own lives also to expect perfection in others – a tendency that can strain relationships and compromise friendships. How do you feel about other people's imperfections?

This story is about someone who has already discovered the wisdom of the amber lights.

A fisherman once sat in the midday sun, gazing out to sea, watching his little fishing boat riding at anchor, and thinking to himself how good it was to sit in the sun with no worries, watch the waves breaking and enjoy God's creation.

But his daydream was interrupted when a smartly dressed and rather overweight businessman came up to him and broke into his reverie with a sharp question: 'What are you doing lazing around at midday? Why aren't you out fishing?'

Somewhat taken aback, the fisherman replied, 'I've done my day's fishing. I've taken my fish to market, and now I'm relaxing in the sun.'

'But why don't you put out to sea again and catch some more fish?' his questioner insisted.

'Why would I want to do that?' replied the fisherman politely.

'Well, then you would make twice as much money.'

'Why would I want to do that?'

'Well, then you could buy a bigger, better boat, and catch even more fish. You could even employ other

> *people to do the fishing. My word, you could own a whole fleet of fishing boats if you weren't so lazy.'*
>
> *'Why would I want to do that?'*
>
> *'Well, if you owned your own fleet of boats, and employed other people to do the fishing, you would have as much money as you could ever dream of.'*
>
> *'Why would I want that?'*
>
> *'Well, then you could spend the rest of your life just doing whatever you wanted to do, sitting in the sun, relaxing and enjoying yourself, with no worries ... '*

Just imagine if we could learn to live more like the fisherman: we might start a trend. The frenzied folk of the busy world might stop and ask themselves what they are really striving for, and ever so gradually the human family might re-discover the lost art of contentment. But before our imagination runs away with us, let us remember that the trend starts with us.

PAUSE FOR THOUGHT

- In what ways have the amber lights in your life caused you to slow down?
- Wisdom grows best in quiet spaces. How do you make quiet space in your life. What helps you to go beyond the 'strain and stress' in your inner life? How do you help the glass of muddy water to settle so that you can see more clearly?
- Notice any regrets that haunt you about things you will never do again, people and places you will never visit again. Simply notice your feelings

without any judgement. When you have come to stillness, try turning the regrets round into gratitude for the many memories and experiences you have gathered.

- In the story of the race between Enthusiasm and Steadfastness, the competitors grow beyond competition to collaboration. When have you found that taking the slow and steady approach was more fruitful than the fast track?
- How do you feel about the tension between action and contemplation? Have you noticed this in your own life or the life of your friends, colleagues or community? Where does your own strength lie, and how can this find partnership with the strengths of others in a spirit of mutual respect and co-operation?
- How do you feel about the story of the fisherman and his conversation with the businessman? Does it resonate in any way with your own life? Would your choices align more with the attitude of the fisherman or the businessman?
- Has anything we have explored in this chapter caused you to re-visit any aspect of your own lifestyle? Are there any changes you would like to make?

CHAPTER 3

LETTING GO

The soul grows by subtraction, not by addition.
Meister Eckhart

THE PROCESS OF letting go begins in the Maternity Unit and doesn't end until we have taken our last breath. Between these two points come very many times when we have to let go of something – or someone – we love.

If you could remember what your life was like before you were born, you would know that you once lived in the perfect little home in your mother's womb, heated to just the right temperature, with the right food supplied on demand and space that grew with you. All this and the cosy reassurance of your mother's heartbeat. This is hardly a residence that you would have been eager to leave behind. Your mother, meanwhile, had to let go of *you* and she would probably have told you that this was no easy undertaking either.

But your pre-natal idyll couldn't last. The contractions began and you found yourself expelled from paradise. You lost your home. You didn't know where the next meal would come from, and, worst of all, you lost your mum. Or so it would have seemed. No wonder you cried. As for mum, she expelled you from your comfort zone, in the midst of extreme discomfort herself. It would have felt like loss and pain all round, but of course it was the beginning of a whole new life, quite literally. If she were here today she might also share with you that subsequent separations from you were also painful, when, for example she had to leave you at the school gates on your first day at school, or when she watched you go into the arms of a future life partner, hoping and trusting that you would find happiness.

You would soon learn that, although you had lost your womb-world, you had entered into all the beauty and wonder of our living planet. You exchanged the placental food supply for every kind of feast that you would enjoy through the years. And far from losing your mum, you had entered into a different kind of life that would open up a much more fulfilling relationship with mum and with many other people who would touch your life, and whose lives you would touch, with love. What appeared to be devastating loss turned out to be amazing gain.

If a baby had the choice to stay for too long in the comfort zone of the womb, it would die. The same is true for the mother. If she could prolong the pregnancy too far beyond its natural course, she too would be in mortal danger. Nature herself insists that we may not, and cannot cling to any material thing, however much we cherish it, but, ultimately, have to let it go, and move on to embrace the future and all it may bring. In his poem *Eternity,* William Blake gives us due warning:

He who binds to himself a joy
Does the winged life destroy;
He who kisses the joy as it flies
Lives in eternity's sun rise.

This doesn't, of course, mean that every experience of loss in our lives will lead to the discovery of something even better, but sometimes it will be so, in ways we could not have expected. Perhaps you have memories of having to let go of something you loved and found, later, that the subsequent gain far outweighed the loss?

Could it be that the experience of loss that is intensified by the passing of the years might in some respects be the gateway to a new way of being the person we truly are? Living our wisdom years mindfully, and with gratitude rather than with regret, is a pathway through and beyond this gateway. We will explore some aspects of this potential in a later chapter, as we unwrap our 'winter gifts'.

LOSING OUR ILLUSIONS

We never choose to lose what we value. As the years advance we discover that loss is definitely on the agenda. Some losses, however, are actually necessary to our spiritual growth. These are the events that cause us to lose our *illusions.*

So much is becoming more fragile, less reliable, in our troubled world, and this is especially apparent in our later years. As we mature we realise that much of what we had assumed would never change has gone. Think of some of the things we have, for so long, taken for granted, and how it feels when they disappear ...

- Our health, mobility and independence.
- The security of a steady and comfortable income.
- Our faculties (sight, hearing, even mental capacity) and our memory that can so easily let us down in the most embarrassing moments.
- Our status in the world and the affirmation that we are 'useful' members of society.
- Our freedom to choose (for example, where we live and who with).
- Friends who move away or die, and children who fly the nest.
- The freedom of movement that comes from being able to drive a car safely.
- Competence to tackle new technology and manage our lives in an increasingly complex and fast-moving world.

Where is the blessing in all of this? We are becoming disillusioned. But can this be a gift?

The gift, the blessing, is precisely in the loss of our *illusions.* We have lived long and seen much and maybe we have become a bit cynical. We will certainly have lost many of our illusions, but there are some that resist the shedding, especially those that we don't yet realise we still have. How do you feel about some of these commonly cherished illusions?

- That youth, attractiveness and energy will last for ever
- That political leaders mean well with us
- That public figures are honest
- That I am in control of my own destiny
- That I am strong and independent

- That friends and family will never fail me, or I them
- That my country is always right
- That life is fair
- That technology is reliable and progress is always a good thing
- That the climate is stable
- That peace is guaranteed.

Perhaps most of us harbour two unconscious, and conflicting illusions: first, the illusion that we are the 'good guys', basically nice, likeable and a force for good; and, in complete contradiction, the illusion that our presence in the world is insignificant, we can do nothing to change anything, and have nothing to contribute.

Marianne Williamson, in *A Return to Love*, suggests this challenging view of these two illusions: *'Our deepest fear is not that we are inadequate. Our deepest fear is that we are powerful beyond measure. It is our light, not our darkness that most frightens us.'*

The truth between these two illusions is that we have a huge potential for good, but we have not yet arrived.

What illusions have you lost? How do you feel about this loss? And how do we discover any illusions we are still unconsciously cherishing? Often it will be some shock event or conversation that awakens us to a new understanding, for example when something we had always assumed to be unassailably true is challenged in ways we can't ignore, and dormant illusions are painfully stirred into consciousness.

Illusions are a bit like addictions. We get hooked to them and begin to construct our lives and our choices around them, and only when we are cut down can we move on with some of the scales removed from our eyes. The more scales that are removed like this, the clearer our sight becomes. Our expectations are adjusted to reality. When we cling to our illusions we are not standing on solid ground. When we lose them, we feel the drop painfully, but we are freed to walk on, in a greater sense of truth. The scales are a bit like cataracts. Many people have them as they grow older, and many are amazed at how much more clearly they see the world when they are removed.

LETTING GO OF THE ASSUMPTIONS AND EXPECTATIONS OF OTHER PEOPLE

A good friend, passing his eightieth birthday, once said how glad he was that he no longer needed to worry so much about what other people were thinking. You may not share this level of relaxation – most of us are rather more concerned about the opinions of other people than we like to imagine. But my own experience has been that we no longer lie awake at night racked with anxiety about our 'image' as perhaps we did as teenagers. When we are no longer in paid employment we don't have to conform ourselves to the demands and expectations of an employer. (It was a rather amusing side effect of working from home during the COVID lockdowns and communicating only via our computer screens that we discovered that we could go to work meetings or deliver presentations in our pyjamas, provided we wore something a bit more acceptable from the waist up.)

It's a gift to be old enough not to care too much about what the world thinks of us. It's a gift to let go of tasks that have been imposed on us for whatever reason when we realise that life is too short to let it be filled up with other people's demands or the expectations imposed by a flawed and fickle society. It's a gift, that often comes in the wake of a serious loss or perhaps even a bereavement, to be able to distinguish between what really matters to us and what can be let go.

It may also be time to let go of some of the expectations we place upon ourselves. The wisdom years can teach us the difference between bearing one another's burdens and carrying one another's baggage. It will always be part of our responsibility as human beings to be mindful of our neighbours' needs, but this doesn't mean picking up their baggage and solving their problems. We are not helping another by carrying their baggage, in fact we are impeding their growth, just as doing your children's homework isn't helping them to learn, but actually hindering the learning process. Wisdom helps us to recognise the difference between the burdens that we can and should help to carry and the baggage that the person concerned needs to handle for themselves.

LEARNING NOT TO CLING

A work course I once attended was held in a place, and at a time, that I realise, in hindsight, coincided with something of a spiritual growth spurt for me. When the course ended I was very reluctant to leave. The days spent there had been so fruitful for my inner life, regardless of the technical information I had been sent to study. On the last morning I roamed the grounds one last time, wishing – perhaps even praying – that the experience might never end. This happened many years ago, but I have never forgotten the response I felt arose to that unspoken wish-prayer. If I can put this into words, it would sound like this: 'Don't cling to the blessing you feel you have received here, but walk on with empty hands. There are many more gifts waiting for you in the future, and you can only receive them with empty hands. Don't be afraid to let go of what you have received, because it is already safely stored deep within your heart, and can never be lost.'

That was the day I learned the importance of empty hands – so counter-cultural in an acquisitive society, but so essential to our spiritual growth and a key milestone along the road to wisdom.

The Christian story tells how on Easter Sunday, Mary Magdalene was wandering disconsolately round the garden tomb where her friend Jesus had been buried, when she saw the gardener coming towards her. Imagine her joy when she realised that the gardener was in fact the risen Jesus. Small wonder that she flung her arms around him, thinking, perhaps, 'Thank goodness this was all a terrible dream. My friend is alive. Now we can go back to how things were.' Jesus releases himself from her embrace and tells her gently: 'Don't cling to me.' We might imagine him going on to say, 'Don't cling to what has been, but walk with me towards all that shall become.'

The fulness of the future requires us to stop clinging to the past.

LETTING GO OF CERTAINTY

It's very hard to let go of what is familiar and step out into an unknown future. We tend to cling fiercely to what we know, fearing loss, change and the unknown, triggered by a deep anxiety that may go back to childhood, or even back to our ancestral struggles to survive on the savannah. To let go of certainty is to surrender control and recognise that ultimately we do not control our own lives, and most definitely do not have the right to seek to control the lives of others.

One of the hardest truths about life is that nothing is certain. Nothing is guaranteed. There is hardly any human debate upon which the last word has been spoken. If you can imagine life on earth generally, and specifically your own life on earth, as a journey, it can be tempting to think that the circumstances that currently surround us are already the destination. We may think we have arrived, especially if we are in our later years. But if we think we have arrived, we have almost certainly gone down a cul-de-sac, where we risk getting stuck. We think we know how to manage our lives, until we come up against the unmanageable, when all our assumptions unravel. We think we are in control, until life pulls the steering wheel out of our hands.

This can be particularly difficult when it comes to religious belief, which can give us the illusion of sailing towards a safe harbour where we are protected by divine power from the many bad things that could befall us. The wisdom years know that this was never the case. There is no protection from the storm, but there is deep guidance on how best to steer the boat. The freedom to keep growing and evolving will cost us our imagined certainties and compel us to re-focus our vision.

Two incidents remind me of the power of this wisdom. A friend, who was in her quite senior years and old enough to have known better, decided to try surfing during a visit to Australia. She soon fell foul of a big wave that sucked her under water. She clung to her surfboard for dear life, under the illusion that it would somehow keep her safe. She told me later that as she struggled for her life, thinking that her end was near, she thought she ought to have prayed, but instead found herself thinking 'What a stupid way to die.' Eventually her strength gave out and the power of the water ripped the surfboard from her grip. And almost immediately, freed of the board, she floated back to the surface and relative safety.

I too once had an encounter with a rip current while snorkelling on the west coast of Australia. I struggled, in vain, to swim against the current and back to the boat, but the effort was totally exhausting and utterly fruitless. I had to do what I had been taught and raise my hand in surrender, as a signal to the boat to come to my rescue. I was duly fished out of the water, all energy spent, and brought to shore, where I learned from my experienced companions that if you are caught in a rip current you should never try to swim against it, but, if possible, move sideways, out of its path, and call for help. This turned out to be a lesson for life. When caught in serious turbulence, acknowledge your own helplessness to overcome it, step out of the path of the storm if possible, and signal your need of assistance. When we stop fighting the inevitable, we may find that there is a place of deeper peace, where, freed of our illusions, we discover more solid ground.

In reality, everything we have and possess is finite and limited. We cling to it, and fail to understand that in letting it go, we are emptying our hands to receive something much greater. A traditional Mediterranean story shows us just how true this can be...

There was once a really old man who had lived a long and happy life on a beautiful island. He loved his homeland very much. He and his family, through all the generations, had made their homes, earned their daily bread and raised their children on the island. And so, when the old man realised that he was approaching the last days of his life he asked his children to take him outside one last time. There he knelt and gathered a handful of his native soil, clutching it tightly with his fingers, and asked to be buried holding the soil in his hand.

Soon afterwards the old man died and came to the gates of heaven. The angels greeted him joyfully. 'You have lived a good life,' they said. 'Welcome to the kingdom of heaven. Please come in.'

So the old man tried to cross the threshold of the heavenly kingdom, but as he did so, a kindly angel said, 'But you must first let go of the earth.'

'Oh no,' said the old man, 'I could never do that. This is my native soil, the earth of my beloved island home.' The angels were sad as they went back to heaven, leaving the old man wandering, lonely, outside the gates.

After a while the angels came again. They brought him a taste of the heavenly banquet and feasted with him there, outside the gates, trying to persuade him to let the earth go and enter the fulness of heaven. He wanted so much to join them but still he couldn't let go of the earth he was clutching. And again they had to leave him standing there, alone.

Many years passed and the angels came again, this time bringing with them the old man's granddaughter, who had been a little girl when he died, but had now grown up, grown old, and died. The old man was so overjoyed to see her again and in his joy he flung out his arms to embrace her. And as he did so, the soil slipped right through his fingers.

And so, after all this time, the old man walked, hand in hand with his granddaughter, into the heavenly kingdom. And what did he find there? The whole of his beloved island, waiting there to welcome him to his eternal home.

We cannot imagine the fulness and the freedom of the 'more' as long as we are clinging to the 'less'. Just as we might light a candle on a dark night to help us see a few steps ahead, but when daybreak comes the light of our candle will be totally eclipsed by the full light of the new dawn.

LEARNING FROM THE TREES

In the autumn the deciduous trees let their leaves fall. Imagine how it would be if they had a choice. They might decide to cling on to their leaves, especially when they are at their glorious best, radiating rich colour throughout the forest. What would happen if they could make such a decision? Well, they might be able to hang on to some of their leaves but not for very long, because winter is already hovering in the wings to claim them. It's also a fact that the energy levels of the tree are dropping, and nature directs the remaining available energy away from the leaves and into the roots, to ensure that next year there will be another springtime, and another generation of fresh leaves.

What about ourselves? We are in the autumn of our lives. Our 'leaves' are beginning to fall. Some of our pet projects, sporting ambitions or travel plans for example, are beginning to look unattainable. We are having to learn to step back from some of our activities. And our energy levels are certainly dwindling. Unlike the trees, we do have choices about where to direct the limited energy we still have. Will we try to keep all our projects going? Or will we learn from the wisdom of the trees and direct our remaining energy into the roots of our being? What might this mean in practice? Perhaps a gradual move away from excessive action and towards a bit more contemplation, or a change of focus away from the pressures of work and towards the presence of friends and family. There is no right answer to this of course. Each of us must find our own balance as we move forward along Wisdom's way.

The trees will have more to teach us, as we move on to explore the gifts that the wisdom years will bring.

PAUSE FOR THOUGHT

- Take time to reflect back over your own experience of loss. Have any of the losses in your life actually opened up possibilities of new growth or an expanded vision?
- What was the most precious thing you have ever had to let go? How do you feel about it now? Did your letting go make space for some new gifting in your life?
- 'Letting go' is an inevitable aspect of growing older, but can it also bring deeper wisdom? In what ways have you come to understand that 'more is less' in your own experience?
- Sometimes the losses in our lives involve the loss of our illusions. In what ways would you say that you have become 'disillusioned'? Which specific illusions do you feel you have, perhaps painfully, had to lose as your experience of life has widened and deepened?
- Is there anything in your life to which you are still fiercely clinging? Sometimes we cling so stubbornly that only a shock event can shake us free of our unhealthy need for what we cling to. Has this ever happened to you?
- If your home were on fire and you could only rescue very few cherished items, what would you most want to save? This exercise can help you to recognise what really matters most in your life.
- One of the hardest things to let go is our very human need for certainty and control. Have you

had to surrender any of your earlier assumptions and imagined certainties in order to be free to keep on growing into the best person you can be?

- The ultimate letting go in this life is our own death. Does the story of old man and his island help you to trust the dynamic that loss can be the gateway to much richer gain?

CHAPTER 4

WINTER GIFTS

In the final loss of everything that once was sure,
there is also the birth of something new.
Belden Lane

IT CAN BE very hard to live through the many losses that our older years bring. To think otherwise is, frankly, to be in denial. The losses are real, and they are painful.

When Princess Diana died so tragically, and so young, her brother, Earl Charles Spencer, speaking at her funeral, said that she had been taken from us 'at her most beautiful and radiant'. These words, so true of Diana, made me think of the way Nature does exactly this in our woods and forests. A walk through the autumn woods can leave us breathless with delight at the glorious colours of the dying leaves. People travel for hundreds of miles to be present to this season and to rejoice in the colours of the fall – because 'fall' is what it is. Soon these leaves, just as they are at their most beautiful and radiant, will be torn from their branches to lie crushed and helpless on the forest floor.

It all looks like bad news, and the inevitable loss of our own former youth and vigour can feel like that too. But, of course, this is never the end of the story. Like the trees, we have known our life's springtime, with its urgent new growth and rising sap. We have lived through our blossom time, when we were unfurling like flowers, and attracting others to our side. All too soon the flowers faded and fell, having fulfilled their role in our life cycle, and now autumn has come to take their place. Our leaves are falling. So many of our plans and projects have either been completed or abandoned. What has been done has been done. What has not been done, has not been done. Can we let it be?

There's nothing we can do to resist the falling of our life's leaves, or at least not for very long. But the next phase of our lives is revealed when – and only when – the leaves fall, because this is when the fruits become apparent. As we wander through the forest we hear the crunch of beechnuts beneath our feet. We see the squirrels gathering acorns. We rejoice in the burnished bronze of the chestnuts. We gather the fallen apples and harvest the pumpkins. Why would the human race alone be excluded from this annual rhythm?

The poet John Keats called autumn the 'season of mists and mellow fruitfulness'. If we think of our older years as the autumn of our lives, we can readily recognise the 'mist' – the failing faculties and foggy memories, not to mention the appointments with the opticians and audiologists. But what about the 'mellow fruitfulness' that, in the natural world, accompanies the loss of the leaves? We are no less a part of the natural world than the trees. In this chapter we will take a look at the fruits – the gifts that we recognise only when the blossom has faded and the leaves have dropped to the ground. We will take time to notice and celebrate some of the gifts that our 'winter years' bring.

THE GIFT OF HOLY FORGETTING

Can forgetfulness ever be a good thing? Let's look at some of what we may have already forgotten and see how we feel about it now.

Old hurts and resentments. None of us will have come this far in life without getting hurt. Some of those hurts will fester in our memories. Others will have been forgotten. Hurts can't just be pushed under the carpet. They need to be acknowledged and worked through, and then, when the issues that gave rise to them, have been addressed, they need to be laid to rest and forgotten. Our later years can be the space in which we become more mellow, more forgiving, more insightful.

Old, perhaps inherited, prejudices and enmities are also in the gift of holy forgetting. As we grow older, and wiser, we begin to see the world in colour vision, rising above the black and white attitudes that we all too easily adopted when we were younger. We become less dogmatic, more open to see the many other sides to most stories. We move beyond 'my way or the highway' to a recognition that there are many other lanes and by-ways on the way towards truth than our own favourite route.

Of course, this gift only grows in the lives of those who are open to change and modification. We know that it is possible to 'grow' in the opposite direction, becoming more entrenched in hardened attitudes. The choice is ours. How fertile is our heart's soil for welcoming and sustaining the gift of holy forgetting?

THE GIFT OF PEACE-MAKING

The longer we live, the more expansive our view of life becomes – or at least that's the theory. As we look back over our lives we can perhaps see ways in which our attitudes and opinions have become less polarised. This is in stark contrast to the times we are living through, in a dangerously polarised world. Is there a responsibility on us, as elders, to work against such polarisation that is constantly setting one group of us against another, apparently irremediably divided by opposing opinions and ideologies? But how might we hope to do this?

The secret, I suggest, lies in finding common ground. I lived for several years during the Cold War literally in the shadow of the Berlin Wall, hearing the sound of shots and explosions every night. The border territory between the then East and West Berlin was patrolled by killer dogs and sown with landmines. It was, in every sense, a no-man's land. It was inhuman. It was opposed to life itself. By contrast I remember visits to local fairs and community celebrations, where people gathered as human beings, sharing a common desire to enjoy this time together. Transforming no-man's land into common ground is, of course, rather harder than organising a village fair, but it works on the same principle.

I was once confronted, at the start of a retreat focusing on human and spiritual evolution, by one fundamentalist participant who, she said, had come to put me right on my (in her view) flawed understanding of evolution. There was no obvious meeting point between us and I was at a loss to know how the retreat would proceed, given that her opinions were in direct opposition to those of everyone else there. I had a private chat with her, during which she happened to tell me about an aspect of her personal circumstances that resonated strongly with something I had experienced myself. Nothing much needed to be spoken. We met each other in a shared memory of pain and loss. Our differences regarding evolution ceased to be the barrier they had appeared to be and we connected at a deeper level. Our common ground proved to be very much more fertile than our opposite opinions on our human ancestry.

The ability to find and nourish common ground is one of the gifts of our mature years. It can also be a gift for our families and communities, because it is a crucial key to peacekeeping and conflict resolution. And it can apply just as much in global conflicts, if only it were practised.

There was a tipping point during the First World War on Christmas Eve 1914. British troops were surprised by the sight of candles and makeshift Christmas trees appearing along the German trenches, and the sound of carols being sung by the German soldiers. They responded by singing carols of their own, and soon the opposing troops were playing football in no-man's land and exchanging small gifts and photos. Common humanity. Common ground. Tragically it triggered a clampdown by the generals. Once you have found common ground with another human being you can't kill them. That couldn't be tolerated.

If conflict can cease for a Christmas Day, why can't it cease for every day? How different our human story would be if we could focus on the common ground in which we are all rooted. This can begin when we exercise the gift of reconciliation that our wisdom years offers.

THE GIFT OF SIMPLIFICATION

Although external circumstances certainly seem to get more complex as we age, there is also often a natural desire to simplify our lives. This can be driven by the very necessary consideration we need to have for those who come after us, and especially for those who will have to clear up all our goods and chattels when we are gone. There comes a time when we truly don't want any more 'stuff'. We have arrived at the season of our lives when we are trying to shed possessions, not acquire any more.

Sometimes the clutter in our lives is invisible, but can be even harder to clear. Is your spiritual life getting over-complicated? Does it sometimes feel as though the language of creeds and doctrines is a long way from the message of the man from Galilee? Are there any aspects of your faith practice that you now feel the need to move on from? How do you feel about this?

If I needed more convincing about the value of clearing out accumulated clutter this came when I was visiting a dying friend to bring him and his wife communion. We sat at their kitchen table, with a Bible and a lighted candle. I had just begun reading the Gospel when the candle flickered and went out. It was a shock – a painful reminder that my friend's life would also soon be extinguished. I hesitated, wondering whether I should pause the reading, while his wife, equally uncertain, wondered whether she should interrupt the reading to re-light the candle. While we hesitated, my friend himself quietly reached out, lifted the candle and poured off the molten wax in which the flame had drowned. As he set the candle upright again the flame leapt up. Not a miracle, simply what candles do when they are drowning in their own wax, but for us, that morning, a timely promise that perhaps my friend's life, about to be extinguished, would also leap again into a new form of life.

Perhaps your own life feels flooded, either materially or spiritually, or both? Can you pour away the molten wax and let the flame rise again?

THE GIFT OF BRIDGE-BUILDING

In a polarised society, wisdom cries out for new solutions to intractable hostilities. We see antagonism spreading like a virus across the planet, and feel helpless to stem the tide. Some people feel called to engage in active protest, even in their later years, believing that old age should be about doing as much as possible to resist the drift towards being 'useless'. They will 'die in action'. Others are better at stillness. I once observed a particularly unpleasant quarrel involving several angry people. There was a lot of shouting, but one person, a young woman, sat still in the middle of the raging argument, simply holding the stillness. She was a centre of peace in the eye of the storm.

There is no right and wrong here. The activists are doing fantastic work that absolutely needs to be done. But so are the ones who are able to hold the still point in perfect balance while the turmoil rages around them. What they are doing – or rather how they are being – is essential. It is their presence, not their action, that is working here.

Wisdom's secret is to be the balance point between apparently irreconcilable opposites. This is never going to be about compromise. You could say it is the simple change in point of view, from 'either/or' to 'both/and'. The world needs both activists and contemplatives.

The poet-mystic Rumi captures the truth of it like this: *'Out beyond ideas of wrongdoing and rightdoing there is a field. I will meet you there.'*

One of the gifts of our winter years may be the key to the location of this field. Elders often have a special gift for building bridges in families and communities.

A story shows us how, through our own attitudes, we can turn barricades into bridges:

There was once a farmer whose land bordered on that of a rather unfriendly neighbour. They had once been friends, but they had quarrelled bitterly and now would have nothing to do with each other. One day he woke to find that his neighbour, out of sheer spite, had dug a deep trench between them so that they would never be able to cross over the boundary. So angry was the farmer that he called in a carpenter and asked him to erect a high fence between them, so that he would never have to see his neighbour, or the ugly trench that divided them.

The farmer went to market for the day. When he came home he was shocked to see that the carpenter had used the fence posts he had provided, not to erect a fence but to build a bridge right across the trench.

The carpenter had even decorated the bridge with intricate carvings depicting scenes from the two farmers' previous friendship. The farmer was about to complain to the carpenter when he noticed his neighbour tentatively crossing the bridge, head hung low, hand outstretched.

'I'm sorry for my spiteful action in digging this trench,' said the neighbour. 'And now you have created this beautiful bridge as a sign of friendship instead of enmity and revenge. Can we now shake hands, let bygones be bygones, and from now on not be just neighbours but also friends as we used to be?'

The Berlin Wall divided the citizens of the city (and indeed of the country and the world) for 28 years, severing families, friends and lovers. When it was demolished in 1989, much of it was turned into material for road-building, and it is said that this was the best road-building material ever.

Barriers can become bridges. Road blocks can become freeways. Cold wars can become warm friendships. Maybe it can begin with you and me.

THE GIFT OF PATIENCE

You may think you missed out on this one? I certainly only got a half portion, but I'm grateful for that, and maybe it will grow as I mellow.

Try looking back to your youth. Those were the days (long before credit cards) when debt was very much a no-no, except for the bigger purchases like houses and cars. Back then if you wanted something you would normally have had to save up for it. It was the age of piggy-banks and half-crown birthday presents (for any younger reader that amounts to 12.5 pence in today's currency, but it would have gone rather further in the forties and fifties, probably equivalent in value to about £1.50).

Today the art of waiting and saving seems to have gone out of fashion, but wisdom reminds us that our more frugal habits were no bad thing. They brought us an anchor point of stability and financial responsibility, making it possible to achieve some of our long-term dreams, including, perhaps, being able to help the younger generation along the rocky financial road.

A friend of mine told me a true story about her own niece. The child was out shopping with her mother one day, and she spotted a doll that she wanted. She asked her mother to buy her the doll, and the mother, wisely, refused. The child, however, would not take 'No' for an answer, and kept pestering her mother for the doll. The mother continued to refuse but made a suggestion: 'If you really want the doll so badly, you could ask Santa for it when Christmas comes round.' The child wasn't having any of this, however. She stamped her feet, 'But Santa knows I need it NOW', she retorted.

We have learned, through our long years, that life doesn't deliver our wants and wishes on demand. We have learned to wait, and usually to save, for what we need or desire, and, dare I suggest, as a result we have learned to cherish these things more because of the effort we, or others, have made to obtain them. This is the gift of delayed gratification and it isn't something our society values any more. Now, with hindsight, I would rate the gift of patient waiting to be more precious than the material objects I thought were so important at the time.

THE GIFT OF TOLERANCE

Another gift that you, like me, may feel you missed? Some of my own intolerances relate to language. For example, I don't like the use of the word 'kids' (and even worse 'grandkids') to describe young children. On one occasion I was preaching this particular gospel to my (then very) young granddaughter. 'Kids', I told her, are young goats, and children are not goats.' Imagine my dismay when, a few days later, she announced to her parents over dinner that 'Grandma says children are goats.' My determination to get the English right had actually implanted a completely false idea in her young mind, as she tried to untangle my logic and had reached entirely the wrong conclusion. It made me question just how important it really was to make the world conform to my own idea of correct English.

It has, however, taken a lifetime to defuse some of my many other intolerances and to begin to realise that just as the faults and foibles of others annoy me, so my own faults and foibles are an irritation to them. But it's a slow process, and I'm far from finishing the journey.

A student I once knew helped a group of us in the university chaplaincy along the path to greater tolerance. After graduation she joined an order of silent enclosed nuns and she used to send letters back describing her experience. In one such letter she told us that 'recreation hour' was the hardest time for her. 'I sit in the circle with my sisters,' she confessed, 'thinking to myself how much easier convent life would be if

Sister A were not in it. After mentally removing Sister A from the circle, I realise then that Sister B is also very irritating. By the end of the hour I have mentally eliminated all the sisters, from A to Z, from the circle. And then I am left with one last question. Where is the problem now?' I think we could all identify with her dilemma.

One piece of wisdom I picked up along the way is this: when you point a finger at someone else, remember there are three fingers of your hand pointing back to yourself. I have also come to recognise that there are very many different opinions about almost everything, not only my own – and some of them may even be right!

THE GIFT OF EMPATHY

An elderly relative lived with us for several years. At the time I used to get impatient because she always wanted a bright light by which to do her sewing and mending and I preferred a soft light. We didn't fall out about it, but it has taken me years – decades in fact – to reach the point in my life when I too need a brighter light to read by while the younger family members prefer a softer light. Now, when it is too late, I have great empathy with our house guest from back then. Too late to apologise for my intolerance. But not too late to discover the importance of empathy.

Empathy, I suggest, is also one of the winter gifts that comes when we know in our own lives something of what another person is going through, whether suffering or celebration, grief or joy. This can be a unifying experience that bonds us more profoundly with each other. To truly feel a deep emotion with another, we have to have felt it ourselves. Only then does their pain connect with ours, their joy with ours.

Sympathy is relatively easy, and can be dispensed in words. 'Feeling for' another person asks only a kindly attitude. Empathy is harder, and deeper, and it springs from shared experience. What we have experienced ourselves draws us to truly 'feel with' the other, so that their pain becomes in some way joined to ours. Life has given us the experience. If our heart's soil has been sufficiently softened, it will transform that experience into compassion.

THE GIFT OF BEING WHO YOU ARE

Some older people find that they are no longer so concerned with what other people are thinking. Of course such concerns never completely go away, but the passing of the years can take the edge off the anxiety that they create. We have reached the age when we are more comfortable in our own skins. We no longer have anything to prove.

A story is told about a young man who was very impressionable and hated to cause a fuss. One day he went to a famous tailor, to order a new suit. The tailor took all the necessary measurements and invited the young man to come back in two weeks for the first fitting. It didn't go very well. The young man pointed out, very tentatively, that the trousers were ill-fitting, and would make him have to walk like a crab. The tailor dismissed the complaint.

The second fitting arrived, and this time the jacket didn't sit properly on his shoulders. It would, the young man stated, force him to walk bent over to one side. The tailor was getting angry now and told the customer to stop his endless complaining. The final fitting revealed that one sleeve was longer than the other. When the young man pointed this out, the tailor, now losing his patience completely, told the young man to hold the shorter sleeve down with his hand, and then both sleeves would be the same length.

And so it was that the young man paid the tailor, put on the ill-fitting suit, and walked down the road – walking like a crab to accommodate the badly made trousers, shoulders hunched up to adapt to the faulty jacket, and his body bent sideways to hold down the shorter of the two sleeves. The people saw him coming and felt sorry for him. 'That poor young man,' they said, 'but hasn't he got a clever tailor.'

Has life, or contemporary society, put you into an ill-fitting 'suit'? Have you had to adapt yourself to systems that try to conform you to the expectations of others, or of society generally, and mould you out of shape? And have you 'paid the tailor'? (If in doubt, check your tax bill!) It becomes clearer, in our later years, how often we distort ourselves to fit the system, instead of recognising that it is very often the system itself that is distorted. The 'clever tailor' may need to be challenged, not paid.

Let us grant ourselves this gift, which is actually our birthright, to be the person we truly are, and stop twisting ourselves out of shape to meet the expectations of systems (social, political or religious) that are themselves distorted. Better, by far, to change the systems, than to lose ourselves. Be yourself. Everyone else is taken!

THE THING ABOUT GIFTS ...

... is this. They are only effective if and when you unwrap them, open them up and use them. We all receive these 'winter gifts', but we have a choice about whether we will accept them. Like the gardener who was given a packet of seeds. The picture on the packet was of a beautiful flower. So beautiful that the recipient propped the packet up on a shelf and admired it every time she passed. 'How lovely it would be,' she thought, to have a flower like that growing in my garden.' All of the gifts we've considered come in seed packets like that. They will only bloom if we open the packet and spread the seeds in our hearts so that they can grow in our lives.

PAUSE FOR THOUGHT

- Have you discovered a more mellow kind of relationship with anyone who has hurt you in the past?
- Can you name any prejudices that may have driven you in earlier years? Have you modified your opinion since then?
- How have your priorities changed over the years? How have these changes affected the way you now choose to live your life
- As you look back over your life, can you see ways in which your attitudes and opinions have become less polarised over time?
- Do you feel more, or less, tolerant, with the passage of time?
- Have you made any important compromises? How do you feel about them now?
- In your family or community, do you sometimes find yourself helping to resolve conflict? How are you doing this? How might you do it more intentionally? Conflict resolution is often the province of the elders in society.
- Do you feel a need to simplify your life? How will you achieve this?
- What will you let go, and what would be important to keep?
- Is your religious life getting cluttered? Are there now aspects of your faith practice that you need to move beyond? How does this leave you feeling?

CHAPTER 5

INDEPENDENCE?

Peaceful living is about trusting those on whom we depend and caring for those who depend on us.
Dalai Lama

THE LOSS OF independence, and with it the autonomous control of our lives, is something we all dread. In the Christian story Jesus once warned Peter that the day would come when 'someone will put a belt round you and take you to where you did not want to go.' This happens as we get older, beginning with the need to make sometimes reluctant choices about where and how we live, as we adjust to changing circumstances. It will often involve decisions about whether, and for how long, we can continue to drive safely before we lose this aspect of our independent mobility. It can go as far as the prospect of someone having to invoke power of attorney on our behalf.

Is independence as important as we once thought? Is it even real? We began our lives in total dependency. We longed for independence and eventually attained it, or thought we did, as we reached what we called maturity. And that's where many people end their journey – proud of the independent lives they have achieved. We will all be familiar with the fantasy of the 'self-made man'.

In this chapter we will explore two possibilities:

- That there is no such thing as independence, and our need for friends, family and community reveal our deep need for each other, and the whole of the natural order, to do almost any task we can imagine, and
- That there is another step beyond independence – this is the growing awareness of our *inter-dependence*.

This is a more mature state of awareness, and one that not everyone arrives at.

We are told that the antenatal development of each physical human life reflects the process of the evolution of all physical life. What if the spiritual development of each of us as individuals reflects something of the spiritual evolution of all humanity? We begin by believing whatever we are told as children, dependent for our understanding on those who teach or influence us. Then we grow into what we think of as independent thought, nourished, we hope, by sound education, but we remain mainly focused on personal survival and success. And finally we begin to understand the reality of inter-dependence calling us to contribute more fully to the greater good of all life. If this pattern of development also reflects the potential spiritual evolution of all humankind, then our destiny on this earth would find its fulfilment in a state of mutual inter-dependence with all created life.

DEPENDENCY

The first, and essential stage of every life finds us, as infants, completely dependent, needing help with every single action. We grow gradually to a less total dependence, but for human beings, this is a slow process lasting for decades. In this state of dependency, we strive, increasingly, to resist our need of others, and to assert our perceived independence. It's generally suggested that this resistance starts to be painfully noticeable in the so-called 'terrible twos' when toddlers can be so determined to have their own way that they can throw furious tantrums when this desire is frustrated.

In later years we dread returning to this state of dependency on others for help in the ordinary acts of life. Once we feel we have mastery over our own lives, we can be extremely reluctant to accept help or advice.

There are some exceptions to our natural drive towards independence, and it's possible to maintain a state of dependency in certain respects into adulthood. In an unhealthy personal relationship, for example, a co-dependency can develop, whereby one partner is dependent on the other's love and attention to the point of addiction, and unduly fearful of losing it, while the other partner can feel trapped or manipulated, but at the same time needing, or even exploiting the other's dependency. Learned helplessness is another way to remain dependent by becoming reliant on other people to solve problems that you would, more healthily, work on solving for yourself.

These kinds of dependency can prevent us from moving forward into healthy adult independence. But is this independence real?

INDEPENDENCE

In fact there is no such thing as independence, although most of us believe we have it. If we imagine ourselves living through a normal day we realise just how little we can actually achieve independently.

Let's test this theory.

You got out of bed this morning and made breakfast. Did you grow the tea leaves you used, or the coffee beans? Did you make your favourite mug from which to drink it? Did you milk the cow or pasteurise the milk or bottle it yourself? Did you grow the oats for your porridge or lay the eggs or make the marmalade, or the jar it came in? Did you forge the cutlery you used? Did you make your own toothbrush or toothpaste, or fix your own teeth last time you needed a filling? Did you make the soap you used or instal the shower or the plumbing pipes?

Maybe you are wishing, now, that you'd stayed in bed, but the day is only just beginning. Did you make the car you drove to work in, or drive the bus, or produce the fuel to make it go? Did you lay the tarmac on the road or design the traffic light system? If you went shopping, how much of what you bought could you possibly have made or grown yourself or packaged and transported to your home?

Evening, and time to put your feet up. Did you design your own television, or write the play you watched, or compose the music in the concert you listened to? Did you even make the chair you sat in. Did you grow your own grapes for the glass of wine you enjoyed, or pick the hops for that cool beer, or harvest the cocoa beans for that naughty little chocolate treat?

Okay, you get the message. Time to sleep in a bed you didn't manufacture, cosy under bedding made of cotton you didn't spin, bathed in moonlight you didn't create. Just how independent are you?

But don't let these thoughts undermine your healthy self-confidence because, however dependent you are on others for the daily necessities of life, there is a hugely important area of your life for which you, yourself, are responsible. This is the matter of your choices. Your freedom and your autonomy lies in the fact that you can choose your attitude and response in every situation and make your choices in line with your own values.

Which brings us to one the most important reasons for desiring independence, because it's in this stage of our development that we are discovering who we are ...

Our desire for independence is partly about a healthy need to discover who we are, and have the courage to be ourselves, rather than being unduly shaped by the expectations of others or of society in general.

How do you balance the healthy need to 'Be Yourself' with your recognition of our mutual interdependence?

There's an Australian story told about the platypus that encourages us to 'be ourselves'. The platypus is a particularly odd kind of creature, combining features that would normally be associated with both mammals, fish and birds. (It is officially scientifically classified as a monotreme mammal.)

See whether the story speaks to you...

Once upon a time there was an inquisitive duck who lived on a pond with all the other ducks, but took off one day to swim down the river to explore the wider world. After a hard day's swim she needed a rest, and settled down on a cosy mound at the water's edge, little guessing that she was actually perched on top of the home of a water rat. 'Ah,' thought the water rat. 'A sitting duck!' and promptly seized the hapless bird and dragged her down into his den where he forced her to become his wife.

Time passed, and the duck was unable to get free of her captivity, until one happy day the water rat fell asleep on the riverbank, and she eagerly grasped the opportunity to flee back to her home pond. The other ducks were very happy to see her again. Springtime arrived and the time came for them to lay their eggs. Our adventurous duck also laid her egg and was as happy as all the other ducks. And in the fulness of time the eggs hatched, but to our duck's dismay, a very strange little creature emerged from her egg, resembling a cross between a rat and a bird. This proved to be too much for the other ducks to tolerate. They couldn't deal with this duckling that wasn't a duckling. They turned on the mother duck and drove her away from the pond.

And now the story moves back to the Australian Dreamtime, when all the creatures were arranging themselves into tribes. First the mammals saw the platypus and eagerly invited her to join them: 'You are clearly a mammal, you are warm-blooded and you suckle your young. Welcome to the tribe of mammals.' 'Thank you friends,' said the platypus,

'I do feel a strong affinity to you and I appreciate your invitation. I'll think about it.' Then came the birds and invited the platypus to join them: 'You are clearly a bird, you have the beak and webbed feet of a bird and you lay eggs. Welcome to the tribe of birds.' 'Thank you friends,' said the platypus, 'I do feel a strong affinity to you and I appreciate your invitation. I'll think about it.' And finally along came the fish with their invitation: 'You are clearly a fish. See how swiftly and gracefully you swim through the water. Welcome to the tribe of fish.' 'Thank you friends,' said the platypus, 'I do feel a strong affinity to you and I appreciate your invitation. I'll think about it.' Finally the platypus told them of her decision. 'I feel close to all of you and I appreciate your invitations, but the truth is: I'm a platypus. And it's okay to be a platypus.'

Discovering who we are, and developing the courage to 'be ourselves' is an important stage in maturing towards true inter-dependence. It would be easier just to go along with the crowd and identify with a group that seems accepting of us, but this can leave us feeling uncomfortable because our real self has not been acknowledged. Our real self is a unique gift that we can offer the world, but we can't offer it until we have found it.

So the quest for independence is a useful, indeed an essential stage along the way. Nevertheless, many people get stuck at this point. Are our wisdom years calling us to journey beyond this stage and grow towards inter-dependence?

THE REALITY OF INTER-DEPENDENCE

In reality, creation is completely inter-dependent. Our thrust for independence can block our growth into this more mature state of life. As we saw in reflecting on how dependent we are in our imagined independent lives, the reality is not a return to infant dependency, but an evolution towards inter-dependence. We depend on so much in the natural world to keep us alive, but we are also mutually inter-dependent on each other, as fellow human beings. This is a much more challenging reality.

With the natural world we have an unspoken agreement. Other living things sharing our mutual planetary home depend on us to care for and cherish that home, and we in turn depend on them and on our planet to sustain us. This, at its best, would be a symbiotic relationship, but it is breaking down. Instead of co-operating with the needs of our planet we have set ourselves into competition with it, taking far more than we need and giving back as little as possible.

The humble butterfly has much to teach us here. As she transforms from a greedy, needy caterpillar into a beautiful butterfly, there is a radical change in her eating habits. No longer the caterpillar's 'grab all you can eat' in the forest takeaway, devouring every leaf in sight, including the one it is sitting on, but now the butterfly's fine dining, the 'sip and savour' at the nectary. The butterfly takes the nectar she needs, freely offered by the open flower, and in return she makes the flower fruitful by gathering and spreading its pollen. This is a symbiotic relationship, a win-win situation benefitting both parties and, ultimately, all creation. This is a demonstration of inter-dependence.

It is also a reminder that life flourishes most fully through co-operation, not competition. Unfortunately our society favours relentless competition and places less value on co-operation. Wisdom asks us to re-examine these values and find ways to live co-operatively, building up community, including international community, rather than seeking greater separation or domination. War is the ultimate outcome of ruthless competition. Peace is the fruit of co-operation. It begins in our own lives and choices.

The full attainment of inter-dependence demands nothing less than that we move beyond our instinct to take for ourselves the maximum advantage and, instead, begin to prioritise the needs of the greater good. It demands that we transcend our individual ego drives and think primarily of the wellbeing of all

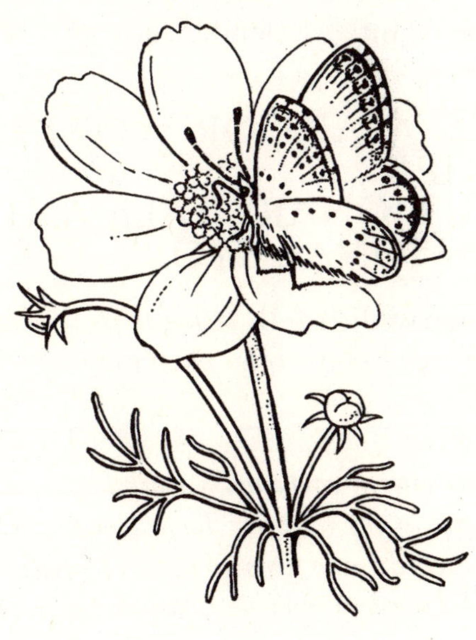

life on earth. This is still a distant dream, but it is a dream that wisdom understands. How do we elders feature in this dream?

Well, think of your relationship with the younger people in your life. They will, mainly, be caught up in the competitive race of life, competing with each other for the best grades, the best job, the most desirable partner. The issues that mainly concern you, however, are not their exam grades or their latest promotion. These things interest you of course, but they are not top of the list of what you wish for them. You are far more concerned with their happiness, their well-being, their hopes, dreams and values. These are the things they are likely to talk to you about, because you can listen, without trying to correct them or preach to them. You have arrived at a longer view, and already begun to live your own life inter-dependently. You have so much to show them, by example rather than by lecturing, about the deeper value of inter-dependence.

PULLING APART OR WORKING TOGETHER … … A CAUTIONARY TALE AND AN INSPIRATIONAL STORY

A traditional Swedish folk story warns of the danger of independence taken to an extreme …

There was once a carpenter's workshop in a small village deep in the country. The carpenter plied his trade peacefully and was always respectful of all his tools. However, one day the carpenter had to go away, and a quarrel broke out among the tools on the workbench. The dispute was about the need, as they thought, to exclude certain members of the toolkit from their community.

'We have to exclude Sister Saw', one of the tools began. 'She bites and grinds her teeth. She has such a peevish nature. She has to go.'

'We can't keep Brother Plane,' someone else joined in, 'He's so cruel and he scrapes everything he touches.'

'And then there's Brother Hammer,' someone added. 'He's so rowdy, never stops his thumping and gets on everyone's nerves.'

'What about the nails,' said someone. 'How are we supposed to work alongside such sharp characters? They are a hazard to us all. And the file and the rasp as well. Living with them is a constant source of friction. And the same goes for Sister Sandpaper, who's so abrasive and is surely the reason for the fractious mood here in the workshop.'

Soon it was a veritable free-for-all, everyone shouting over everyone else, all accusing the others until eventually every tool in the workshop found itself excluded.

Then silence fell. The carpenter had returned. They held their breath and waited for his reprimand. But he said nothing. Instead he picked up a plank of wood. He smoothed it down with cruel Brother Plane and with rowdy Brother Hammer he drove in the sharp, hazardous nails. He picked up rough-natured Brother File and abrasive Sister Sandpaper and made a velvet-smooth finish on the wood.

Every single tool was used by the carpenter to create something new. None was excluded. Each was essential to the task of shaping – a cradle. A cradle to receive a little child. A cradle to hold new life.

By contrast, a traditional Iroquois legend shows us what nature can teach us about the meaning of interdependence ...

Once in a distant field a fine plant grew. Her name was Sister Corn. The summer sun shone down and she grew very tall and strong, but the hot weather dried the earth and her feet began to hurt. She grewnweary, and needed to take more and more strength from the earth, just to stay alive and keep growing.

Another plant grew nearby. She was called Sister Squash and she noticed what was happening. She settled at the feet of Sister Corn to cool the earth and ease her sister's pain by preventing evaporation. However, Sister Corn realised that Sister Squash wasn't getting any of the rainwater that fell so she bent her outer leaves over, to channel some of the precious water down to Sister Squash. In return Sister Squash used her spikiness to keep predators away from them both.

Nearby in the field grew Sister Bean. Sister Bean was weak and unable to support her own weight, so she climbed up the strong stem of Sister Corn. In return she had the special ability to fix nitrogen in her roots to make the soil more fertile for next year's crop, and she helped Sister Corn to stand firm against the days when it was very windy.

When harvest came, each of the three sisters brought her own special gift to the table. Sister

Corn provided carbohydrates. Sister Squash brought vitamins in her fruit and oil from her seeds. Sister Bean brought protein and amino acids. And together, the three sisters brought the world a lesson in how to live and work together in co-operation.

WE ARE ALL IN THIS TOGETHER ...

... whether we like it or not. If we reflect on our various understandings of our origins, they will all lead us to the same conclusion: we are social beings. The Judaic and Christian stories, for example, speak of the creation of two beings because 'it is not good for the human person to be alone' (Genesis 2:18). And if we move to the scientific story, we soon see that we are descended from the apes, who are the most remarkably social creatures on the tree of life. But, as we have already noted, the wisdom years take us beyond the either/or mindset. There is deep truth in all of our origin stories. We don't have to choose between them. But to live together in harmony and raise future generations together, we need to acknowledge our need of each other and our inter-dependence on each other.

Traditional wisdom declares that 'it takes a village to raise a child'. We could also say that it takes a village (or a community) to support an elder. The difference is that the child is not responsible for creating the community that is needed. An elder carries some responsibility for creating and nourishing that mutually supporting community.

In Western cultures the elders frequently have to fend for themselves and are often leading lonely lives, in contrast to other cultures who regard it as the sacred duty of the younger generations to care for the elders. This makes it even more important for those in later years in western countries to work actively to seek and nurture a supporting and mutually inter-dependent community. How do we play our part in this task? Elders have a great track record already for this. So many are expressing the desire to 'give back' to society, honouring all that we have received. There are as many ways of 'giving back' as there are of 'receiving'. Are any of them pulling at your heartstrings?

A traditional Jewish story expresses the simple heart of inter-dependence like this:

A rabbi asked God to give him a glimpse of what heaven and hell would be like. God agreed to this request, and asked the prophet Elijah to be the rabbi's guide on this adventure.

Elijah first led the rabbi into a large room. In the middle of the room was a fire with a big cooking pot bubbling away on it. And in the pot was a delicious stew.

All around the cooking pot sat a crowd of people. They each had a long-handled spoon which they were dipping into the delicious stew. But the people looked pale and thin and wretched. There was an icy stillness in the room. The handles of the spoons were so long that no one was able to get the lovely food into their mouth.

When the two visitors were back outside again, the rabbi asked Elijah what strange place this was. 'That was hell,' Elijah explained.

Then Elijah led the rabbi to a second room, which looked exactly like the first. In the middle, a fire was blazing and a cooking pot was bubbling away, full of the same delicious, aromatic stew. People sat around the fire, with the same long-handled spoons in their hands. But they were enjoying lively, animated conversations with each other.

And the difference? Well, the people in the second room were not trying to feed themselves with the long-handled spoons. They were using the spoons to feed each other. 'Ah, heaven,' said the rabbi.

PAUSE FOR THOUGHT

- In the light of what we have been exploring, how do you feel now about the importance of independence?
- Where do you find yourself in life at present – largely dependent on others, or mainly independent?
- How comfortable do you feel in your own skin, being the unique person you are, not dependent on the opinions of others? Can you also say, like the platypus, 'It's okay to be me'?
- The 'regular' ducks reject the duck in the story whose egg hatches into a platypus. How do you feel about those in our society who diverge in different ways from what society regards as the norm?
- How might you engage with the challenge to help create and nourish community in the place where you live?

- Where do you find examples of the 'hell' of the long-handled spoons story in our western society?
- Are there any examples of 'heaven' in your own locality (for example in your local food bank or mutual support groups)?

CHAPTER 6

COMING DOWN THE MOUNTAIN

~

We can make sorrow and suffering into a compost out of which the roses of joy can grow.
Satish Kumara

MY LAST SERIOUS hill walk with the family was, shall we say, memorable. We took the ferry one summer's day over to the Isle of Arran, all in fine fettle. The path up Goat Fell, Arran's highest hill, begins not too far from the ferry terminal. We embarked on the hike in a burst of collective energy, with Oscar the Labrador bounding ahead and walking five miles for every one of ours.

The ascent posed no particular problems, in fact we overtook several groups of walkers on the way up. I even recall feeling grateful (if not a little bit triumphant) that in my mid-seventies I could still climb a mountain at a reasonable pace and arrive at the summit without mishap.

Once on the summit we came across a group of people celebrating the life of a loved one and scattering their ashes in memory. We shared a moment of silent respect with them. In hindsight, it was perhaps a sign of things to come, a reminder of utter vulnerability even when we think we are on top of the world.

All might have been well, had we decided to descend the mountain by the same route, but we had spotted an alternative route on the map, through a less frequented valley, and we set off in that direction instead. Well, as those who walk the hills, or even those who climb the stairs will know, coming down is harder than going up. It challenges a different set of muscles, muscles that may have been in hibernation for a long time and forgotten how to work. And so it was for me.

The path, when we could find it, led across exposed crags to a steep rocky descent that seemed to go on for ever. Half way down my legs went on strike, and kept crumpling beneath me, leading to several undignified falls. My paramedic son-in-law went into full professional mode, restoring me to vertical each time and helping me over the next few metres, while we both battled through clouds of hostile Scottish midges. It became clear that it was going to take a very long time to get back down to the road. So long, in fact, that it looked increasingly likely that we would miss the last ferry home.

Once we were finally down on the road a new problem presented itself. The path we had chosen, it turned out, re-joined the road about five kilometres from the ferry terminal. In the complete absence of either public transport or taxis, we had to hope for help and were soon picked up by a lovely family who piled us, in two instalments, into their car. Thanks to their kindness, we reached the terminal just as the boat was due to depart but there was one more mountain to climb. Between the harbourside and the boat stretched a very long, steep ramp, and there was no way my legs were going to make it up the ramp before the boat was due to sail.

So it was that I finally made my grand arrival at the ferry in a wheelchair, procured by a kindly crew member, who pushed me, somewhat crestfallen, up the ramp, to arrive to a hail of cheers from a jubilant family and a few other curious onlookers.

I share this story with you because it has given rise to some serious reflection, and maybe even a bit of wisdom gleaned that day on the flanks of Goat Fell. Maybe some of these thoughts strike a chord with you too?

First, recognise your limitations! I had to learn, the hard way, that it was unwise to climb a mountain if your legs were not likely to get you down again the other side.

The descent takes you by a route you've never walked before, and brings challenges you didn't expect. We hadn't factored in the exposed terrain, the midges or the vastly increased distance back to the terminal. Coming down life's mountain also brings you through terrain you could not have predicted – terrain that can be harsh and unforgiving and is very different from the path you followed on the way up.

Coming down is harder than going up. Your knees give way because you are physically tired. You are less steady, but your backpack is lighter. Navigating our later years is much the same. It proves to be much harder than bounding through our youth. The strength and energy we thought was forever ours is weakening. Things are no longer as clear and straightforward as we once thought. But (if we have learned to let go of what is no longer necessary) we have less baggage.

As you gradually find yourself disempowered, the realisation dawns that you will need help with some of life's challenges. The sense of helplessness is hard to deal with. It's a new experience. How ready are we to ask for help, or to accept it gratefully when it is freely offered, as it was to us that day on Arran. Asking for help, it is worth remembering, is not about giving up. It's about refusing to give up.

The flipside of our own disempowerment is that it enables others to come to our aid. It empowers them to care for us, help us, offer us the gift of their humanity and strength. If we never needed help from others, others would never realise what gifts they have to offer. Their strength, like ours, won't last for ever. Loving care is a cyclic gift, a flow of positive energy. It asks to be passed on, from the strong to the weak. It asks to be received, by the weak from the strong.

The gradual fading of our own light enables others' lights to shine more brightly. When circumstances render us mute, we can hear more clearly the voices of others.

When we are no longer centre stage, when we step (or are pushed) out of the limelight, there is space for others to have their moment in the sun and for us to recognise and honour what they are bringing to life's stage.

Which, of course, is not to say that we *always* need help. It's important to know when we need and should accept help and when it is wiser to say (gently but firmly) 'Thank you, but no thank you' if we feel others are perhaps disempowering us with intrusive or excessive assistance.

A STORY OF LIGHT IN A DARK NIGHT

A friend surprised us all recently when he announced, in all sincerity, that he had some good news to share. Everyone brightened up. The world news was so utterly bleak that a beam of light shining in the surrounding darkness was more than welcome. And so he told us his good news. First, his old car, that had served him well over many years, had come to the end of its life and had had to go to the scrapyard. He had been a keen cyclist, but his motor-bike was in pieces after a failed attempt to repair it, and he was in any case unable to ride it now, as his health was failing. He had, however, just been given a long-awaited hospital appointment for hip replacement surgery – finally a scrap of good news, we thought. But just as his appointment arrived, so too did his landlord, who needed the property back, and therefore had to ask him to move out.

The shock was palpable around his circle of friends. Yet he was still smiling – really smiling, not a faked effort at happiness. 'And this is why all this is good news,' he went on. And then came the beams of light. Three different friends had offered him a place in their home while he searched for new accommodation. Another had offered to drive him around, now that he had no transport, and yet another came along with the offer to re-build his motor-cycle so that he would be able to sell it. And to add to his delight in getting his hospital appointment at last, someone had offered to stay with him throughout his convalescence. Not least, another friend had given him a practical device to help him put on his socks. There was an expression of genuine joy and gratitude on his face as he expressed his thanks to all the people who had phoned him, emailed him or knocked on his door, all with the question, 'What can we do?'

This is the story of someone who had 'come down the mountain' – a rather steep mountain – and had had the grace to accept help. It's also the story of losing one's illusions. Most of us cherish the illusion of our own continuing good health, the assumption that our possessions are reasonably secure, and that the place where we live is safe. These illusions begin to unravel as time passes. Our health becomes less robust. Our car fails its MOT for the last time. The rumours of 'no fault eviction' begin to spread through the ranks of those who are living in rented accommodation. He didn't ask for any of this, but one freedom remained to him in this crumbling life landscape - the freedom to choose his attitude. He chose to gather the fruits from the fallen tree, and he found they were far more abundant than he could have imagined.

He lost his car, his home and his health. He found

hope for the future, faith in humanity, and friends. They found their strength in his weakness. He found his strength in their love.

A traditional story illustrates how much more we can sometimes see when life knocks us over ...

There was once a country famed far and wide for its holy mountain. People from all over the world had heard about the holy mountain, but the strange thing was, the people who actually lived in the country had a habit of walking around with their eyes always focused on the ground. They never lifted their heads. And if you asked them what they were doing, they would tell you: 'We are searching for the holy mountain, of course. Why don't you join us in the search? This is where you must look.'

And so they lived their lives, restless and moving round in circles, walking up and down the many lanes and alleyways of their country, poring over their maps and arguing with each other about where, exactly, the holy mountain was to be found.

Meanwhile, the holy mountain soared to the skies, waiting patiently for people to discover its beauty and its power, and saddened to watch them picking their way through the world and never stopping to look up.

Then, one day, amid all the hustle and bustle of the people's desperate search for the mountain, one of them fell over, and was almost trampled to death by the milling feet all around him. He lay there, flat on his back, thinking that his end must surely be close, when to his amazement, he looked up and saw the holy mountain towering serenely above him. He tried to tell everyone what he had seen, but no one believed him, so he set off alone to seek out the path that would lead to the mountain.

It was a hard journey, for the path was sometimes steep and perilous, and he kept losing sight of his goal. Many times he fell in his journeying, and every time he fell, he would catch another glimpse of the mountain he was searching for and be encouraged to keep on walking. And as he walked, he noticed that the only other people on the path to the mountain were disabled or sick or were carrying some great load that had made them topple over in their need. He realised that only those who had fallen were ever able to see the mountain, and only those who knew the full meaning of the word 'down' could ever look up.

It is said that a breakthrough often comes about in the solution of a problem when we stop thinking about it. This also applies to scientific discoveries, so we are told. On more familiar ground, have you ever found that you have had to abandon the attempt to recall a name, for example, and that the information you were searching for has floated back into your memory when you stopped trying to remember it?

In our later years life will have a habit of knocking us over through various forms of loss and diminishment. Might these 'downfalls' be an invitation to look up, through the mists of helplessness, to glimpse a bigger vision?

It was a situation like this that afflicted the entire world during the COVID-19 pandemic in 2020. The virus knocked us all out of action and sent us into lockdown. There were many consequences, but not least among them was the dawn of a new understanding of what 'key worker' meant. It turned out the most important occupations were not the professions we had usually associated with status, power and prosperity, but the healthcare workers, the teachers and the delivery drivers, the people who grew our food and made sure it reached our homes. Laid low in lockdown, we discovered that what mattered most were friends and family and caring neighbours.

No one wants to be flattened in the march of life, yet this can be the very place from which we gain new insight. Can this help us see beyond some of our fears around the inevitable loss of status and independence in our later years, and adjust our focus to what matters more?

COMING DOWN THE STATUS MOUNTAIN

We probably all heard the warning, in our youth, to 'be kind to the people you meet on your way up because you may meet the again on your way down.'

The story of Max bears out this wisdom. Max had been a soldier in the German army in the First World War and had seen terrible things in the trenches. When the Second World War broke out he was too old for military service, and served instead in the German equivalent of the Home Guard, firefighting by night and working as a factory foreman by day. Germany was under the Nazi dictatorship and the factory where Max worked used slave labour – girls brought in from occupied Eastern European countries to form a captive workforce. Max soon noticed that the girls had very little to eat and some were in very poor health. He made it his business to procure small paraffin cookers for them to heat a pan of soup for themselves when the Nazi overseers weren't looking, and he found hiding places for the sick to rest in safety.

At the end of the war the Soviet army marched in from the East and liberated these slave workers, bringing them out of the factory, followed by their employers, now shamed and heading for prison camps themselves. Max was among them, but when he came out the girls called out: 'No. Not him. He was kind to us.'

Max had never had an easy life. He was never 'on the way up' in society, but his life motto was: 'In every human situation, stay human.' A man of wisdom, from whom we have much to learn. I'm proud to say that Max was my grandfather-in-law.

And thinking of ladders, I recall another piece of wisdom I once heard: 'Before you put energy into climbing the ladder – first check that it's leaning against the right wall.' As elders we may well have realised that some of the ladders we tried to climb were indeed not leaning against the right wall, in other words, not reflecting our true values. Don't waste time climbing a ladder if you don't, deep down, want to be at the top of the wall it's leaning against. Don't waste time on regrets, however, just notice what you have learned and be selective about where and how you invest your (diminishing supply of) energy.

Our own days of climbing up the ladder of life are over now, if they ever existed. In our western society, any status we may have enjoyed in our lives is unlikely to be ours today. We are no longer 'economically productive'. We may feel that we are tolerated rather than valued by our fellow citizens.

As we, inevitably, make our descent from the mountain of life, we will shed much of our baggage, along with things we have valued. Perhaps one of the hardest things to fall out of our backpacks is our pride. It is very uncomfortable, for example, to lose our social status as homeowners if we have to give up our homes and move into more sheltered accommodation. It can be mortifying to come up against our ignorance when confronted by new technology, if we have been professionally competent and respected in our working lives. It helps to realise that this is the pain of our ego shrinking. This doesn't make it any less painful, but it lends meaning to the pain – it means that we are growing in wisdom, coming closer to the true centre of our being through the shedding of so many external and more superficial layers.

On our way up through the first half of our lives, we carried ambition, strength, enthusiasm, energy, expectations and pride. As we navigate the descent through the second half of life we leave behind our former status, achievements and acquisitions and our physical strength, but we also shed many of our illusions, and our dependency on the opinions of others. Our ego shrinks, and, ultimately, all we leave behind is the trail of our footprints across the hearts of those whose lives we have touched.

I once watched an interview on television between a well-known Christian presenter and a young woman who was running an orphanage in South Africa, mainly caring for children whose parents had died of HIV/AIDS. He asked her what she hoped to leave behind when her life was over. She thought carefully for a few moments and then replied: 'I hope when I die I will meet my Maker with empty hands, because I hope

I will have spent every gift I have been given. And all I hope to leave behind is just a footprint pointing the way for someone else to care for these orphans.' Here was a young woman with a big heart and a tiny ego, moving on empty-handed, and leaving just her footprint on the land to inspire and encourage those who would follow after her.

A NEW SEASON

When our faculties begin to fail, knowledge slips out of focus and memory lapses frustrate us, can we recognise that this is a change of season? We are leaving the season of achievement and entering the season of surrender. Knowledge, until now in prime position, is yielding to wisdom. We are coming down the mountain.

The backpack is lighter, not just because we have eaten our lunch, but because we have shed some of our excess baggage in ways we have explored in earlier chapters. What we carry now in our backpacks is a story. At the foot of the mountain perhaps, metaphorically speaking, there is a cosy inn – a 'telling-place' – where stories can be shared. We have a story to share. The story of the life-mountain we have climbed, the discoveries we have made about ourselves and the world, the views we have seen, the folk we have met. Round the fire in that little hostelry we hear other stories. It is a gathering place where all stories are listened to and honoured.

Among many other roles, we elders are society's story-tellers. Let our story-telling be generous, and let us generously make space for others' stories. Let our stories offer encouragement and not become, as an elderly friend once wryly remarked, 'an organ recital' of all our various aches and pains. In the winter of our lives let us gather not in regret and recrimination but in celebration of all the wild and wonderful lives we have lived.

PAUSE FOR THOUGHT

- In what ways have you experienced 'coming down the mountain' in your own life? How did it feel?
- Do you recognise any pattern in your life when your own disempowerment gave fresh empowerment to others, or when the dimming of your own light gave others a chance to shine?
- How does the story of the mighty mountain speak to you? Have there been times in your own life when circumstances seemed to knock you over and leave you lying on the ground, painfully aware of your own helplessness and perhaps humiliated by what you perceived to be failure?
- When you reflect back over any times like these, did you learn anything from the experience? Perhaps you gained a new perspective on life? Perhaps you discovered something that you had been quite unable to see when you were too busy searching?
- Have you become aware of any painful loss of status in society? How do you feel about it now, in the light of what we have been exploring?

- How do you feel about Max's wisdom, about staying fully human in every situation, whether you are on the way up, or on the way down the ladder, or maybe have never even been on the ladder? How does Max's story speak to you?
- The story of the young woman and her orphanage reminds us that gifts are for spending, not saving. Some religious traditions seem to stress the importance of being 'saved'. What if the value of being 'spent' were actually more closely aligned to the values and examples of those who have lived their lives like the girl in South Africa? Would you also be able to say, at the end of your life, as she hoped to do, that you have spent every gift you were given, and wish only to leave a gentle, generous footprint on the earth as you go?

CHAPTER 7

THE BIGGER PICTURE

The future belongs to those who believe in the beauty of their dreams.
Teilhard de Chardin

THE JESUIT THEOLOGIAN Karl Rahner (1904–1984) said that 'the Christian of the future will be a mystic, or will not exist.' He added that faith in the future will be experiential – grounded in the lived experience of those who profess it rather than in academic doctrine and dogma.

I wonder how you feel about this statement? Just when we have reached the age when we feel we can settle down and live life at a more measured pace, along comes a challenge like this. What does he mean by 'mystic'? Is he right? And is it even a question we need to address in these, our wisdom years?

So, is it back to the rocking chair, slippers and pipe, or is the call to be a mystic something for us? And surely, after all our reflections so far, we know now that it won't be a question of *either/or*, but of *both/and*. We can be of a certain age (which of course doesn't have to involve slippers and rocking chairs) and still feel the call of Rahner's statement. In fact it may be that our wisdom years are the very best time and opportunity to engage with our inner mystic, even though this may be the last thing we ever thought about.

Mystics? We probably thought that 'mystics' are those few rarefied souls who have advanced so far in the quest for the eternal that they barely have their feet on the earth. If you are from a religious background you can probably name some of them: Teresa of Avila, St John of the Cross, Julian of Norwich, for example, or Simone Weil in the more secular tradition. Whoever they were, we would not think of ourselves as in any way related to such a perceived elite company.

Karl Rahner's statement turns this assumption on its head. He's talking about you and me. Probably, if asked, each of us would come up with a different definition of what we think a mystic might be. One of the many variations might be 'one who sees the distant vision, or even a glimpse of a bigger picture of what it means to be human on planet Earth'.

A story is told about a young boy who was out shopping one day with his mother. They happened to pass a local church that looked rather dreary and dull from the outside, and ventured inside to look around. The boy remarked on the stained glass windows that had looked so dull from the outside, but when rays of sunlight shone through them they seemed to come to life. He pointed to one of them, depicting a human figure, and asked his mother 'Who is that?' She replied, 'That's a saint.' The child was fascinated by this mystery and noticed that the light shining through the window was not only illuminating the figure in the window, but also creating colourful reflections on the stone floor of the church.

Soon after this encounter, the boy was sitting in a religious education class at school. The teacher asked the children 'Does anyone know what a saint is?' The boy's hand shot up. 'A saint,' he said, 'is a person that the light shines through and this makes the stones dance.'

This in itself was surely the observation of a (very young) mystic, one who sees something of the eternal in the events and images of everyday life.

Perhaps it's a simple as that. It's not so much about anything we say or do. It's about letting the light shine through us, bringing the stones of everyday existence to life with vibrant colour. Perhaps being a mystic is simply about becoming translucent – open to the Mystery and allowing it to touch our own lives and the lives of others.

And there is a companion role to that of the mystic. This is the role of the prophet – two sides of the same calling. Just as the term 'mystic' may have become shrouded in the mists of antiquity, so the term 'prophet' may have got stuck in our minds in the form of the Old Testament patriarchs or enigmatic seers, warning the people of dire consequences if they pursue their sinful ways. A more helpful definition of the 'prophet', in the spirit of Rahner's proposal, might be 'one who sees something of the future direction of humankind and the possible hazards ahead'.

In the light of these definitions, what might it mean for us, in our own time and space, and in the experience and enlightenment of our wisdom years, to respond to Rahner's challenge, to see the bigger picture and its implications?

Two creatures from the natural world may offer some insight …

THE BUTTERFLY

Imagine her as she flies over the forest and sees the caterpillars struggling with the caterpillar problems, but unable to tell them that they exist within a much greater reality that they can't yet imagine.

They have no idea what lies ahead for them. For them it's all about feeding and self-defence. But the butterfly sees the bigger picture. She knows that the caterpillar life is not the end of the story. She knows that the forest is not all there is. She knows that just when you think you are hopelessly disintegrating, something amazing may be about to happen. She knows that transformation is possible because she has experienced it. The caterpillars couldn't begin to imagine such a thing.

When you can see the bigger picture, everything changes. Many of the things that once caused you so much anguish are now seen to have been transient irritants that you can hardly remember. You have lived through recessions and economic crises. You know that everything passes and the human spirit survives.

Look back over your life and see for yourself some of the ups and downs, the shocks and surprises that you have lived through. How much can you actually remember? Is any of what seemed so desperate at the time still keeping you awake at night?

A friend in Dublin once told me a story that made me smile. He had been traveling on a Dublin bus, sitting immediately behind two men whose conversation he couldn't help but overhear – a young man who was talking about his struggles with the cost of living and the state of the economy with mortgage interest rates at 6%, and an older gentleman who was listening attentively and sympathetically (but could remember when interest rates were 18%). Eventually the older man turned gently to the younger and said, 'Eh lad, is this your first recession?' He knew there would be many more, and fifty years on the young man would barely remember the details. The wisdom years know that 'this too shall pass', that there will be many twists in the road of life, but the human spirit will survive and prevail.

As an elder, who has reflected on your life journey, you have climbed your mountain. You have seen the view from the hilltop and realised that failure and success both contribute to the full story. In hindsight, you can probably see now that what seemed like failure at the time was also contributing to your life experience and helping you grow in wisdom and understanding. You can see that many obstacles raised their heads along your path but you overcame them, and perhaps the process made you stronger and wiser, for we usually learn more from our apparent failures than from our achievements, more from our struggles than from the easy rides.

Seeing the longer view is not just an abstract dream. It can be very helpful in strengthening and deepening your relationship with friends and family, especially the 'caterpillar generation'. Your ability to see the bigger picture can help the younger people in your life deal better with, and perhaps see beyond, their own crises, and the ups and downs in school and at work or in their relationships.

Next time a younger relative or friend comes over for a chat, notice how your ability to see a broader horizon of life may help them more than either of you can imagine. Without saying very much at all, your presence and understanding can help to set their worries and concerns into a wider context.

Your inner prophet will also very often be able to see hazards that lie ahead, and a gentle diplomatic warning, or even a light-hearted cautionary tale, can go a long way to helping them recognise possible dangers.

THE BOUNDARY GEESE

Geese are great teachers and role models of how to be the best you can be. They fly in flocks, with the breeding pairs in the protected interior of the flock, and the birds we might call the boundary geese flying on the outside edge, guarding the others, and watching the distant horizon. Simply by virtue of their position in the formation, they are able to see where the flock is heading, and also to observe any hazards along the way.

However, flying on the edge is much more demanding, exposed to wind, weather and cold. For this reason the boundary geese take turns on the edge, doing their 'shift' before being relieved by the next shift and returning for respite to the warmer interior of the flock. If one of the flock falls sick, another

goose will drop out of the flock to accompany it and stay with it until it either recovers or dies, when either one or both of them join a different flock to continue the journey.

If it looks as though the flock needs to change course, a few pioneering birds will take the risk of veering away slightly in a different direction This takes courage and resilience, to make a decision and stick with it more or less in isolation, until the rest of the flock eventually get the message and follow the new course, or decide to ignore the warning.

Getting older is something of a similarly exposed place in life. There are a number of parallels between the elder generation and the boundary geese. Our focus too is primarily on the protection and guidance of the younger generations. From experience we know that the journey is unlikely to be without problems and we are ready to help solve them as best we can. Ideally we also support and relieve each other when the strain of the edge begins to wear us down. I belong to a local group who produce and serve a hot lunch once a week for anyone who needs it. It is remarkable how committed these people are to caring for the 'breeding flock' but also how attentive they are to each other's needs. If anyone is needing help or encouragement, it is freely given, and if anyone is sick there is always someone more than ready to be there for them. And if the local council needs to change course to take account of residents' needs, there are always those in the group who will stick their necks out to propose a new direction.

THE FORCE OF OPPOSITION

Unfortunately, as we know from our years of navigating the highways and by-ways of life, not all the energies at work in our lives and our world are on the side of life. Some of them are actively trying to keep us apart, and locked into our own small picture. There are those, including powerful decision-makers and social media influencers, who deliberately foment fear, distrust and exclusion and seek to seduce us away from the vision of the greater good. And there are others who, for example through advertising and marketing influence, actually trivialise our view of life, urging us to focus on the superficial, and shrinking our bigger picture into far too small a frame.

It feels as though these are forces beyond our control, but it doesn't have to be like this. If we live reflectively we will become more practised in noticing the effects of the creative and the destructive energies at work. It is in the power of every one of us to choose to lend our energy either to the positive or the negative movements that are shaping particular situations.

A native American story illustrates this challenge …

> *A tribal elder once told his grandchild a story about the 'two wolves' that live inside every human heart – a 'good wolf' who encourages the positive, life-giving choices we make, and a 'bad wolf' that favours our negative choices. Grandad went on to say that these two 'wolves' are in conflict with each other throughout our lives. 'But which wolf wins?' asked the child. 'The one that you feed,' replied Grandad.*

We feed the positive and help it to grow by giving it our energy and attention. We starve the negative and curb its spread by withdrawing our energy and attention from it. Which energies do we want to grow, and which do we wish we could shrink? Whenever we dwell on the destructive things that are happening around us or indulge in negative interactions either in person or online, we are feeding the negative 'wolf'. When we give our attention to the events and relationships that are helping us and our communities to flourish, we are feeding the positive energies and making a small, but significant contribution to making the world a better place.

LIVING CAUTIOUSLY

A friend made me laugh one day when he told me about a problem he was having with the governing committee of a society he belonged to, when he suggested a new, innovative way of proceeding on a particular issue. The chairman of the committee responded. 'I'm all for innovation, but we've never done this before', as he rejected the proposal.

When it comes to responding to the call of our inner mystic to consider the bigger picture in navigating the journey of life, we do of course have choices. We can say 'Yes', we can say 'No thank you', or, most likely, we can say 'Maybe'.

An incident I once observed both amused and disturbed me. I was driving down to town and had to stop at the junction with a main road. The traffic was fairly light, but enough to require caution. To my amusement I saw two cock pheasants fighting in the middle of the main road. Whatever the cause of the conflict, they were totally engrossed in their battle, each intent on wounding the other. Neither of them had any sense of the real and present danger of them both being flattened by the next car to come along the road. It was just a silly incident, but it was also a lesson about human life. How easily do we also become embroiled in the matter of the moment, and completely lose sight of both the threats and the promises that surround us?

A traditional Sufi story warns us about what happens when we become so engrossed in the 'small story' that we lose sight of the bigger picture..

There was once a forest of trees, each living a full life in its own way. But in the natural order of things, over time each tree grew old and eventually died. Meanwhile, various swarms of bees had made their nests in the hollow tree trunks, where they lived happily and produced their honey, and the honey of each different swarm was subtly different in flavour from that of the other swarms.

Then, one by one, the trees began to die and fall.

The bees debated the meaning of this and decided it must be a reflection of the merits of the bees who lived in each tree. Some believed that if a tree fell, the bees in that tree were being punished for a failure in true belief. Others, feeling compassion, tried to help the bees who had become homeless by sharing their own nests. Others pronounced that the homeless bees had clearly been flawed from the very beginning and were predestined to lose their tree and die.

But finally all the trees died and all the bees were homeless. Each group was shocked. All had thought that the trees were about the bees, and failed to see the wider reality of the forest or respect its nature. All had believed that their group was the one true hive, destined to be saved and to establish a new age. None had realised that they all lived in the uncertainty and precariousness of a changing, evolving world, and that each was called to complete its own particular task and then move on to another forest. None had looked beyond its own life or been able to see itself as part of a greater reality.

LIVING ADVENTUROUSLY

Judaic scripture tells an extraordinary story about an elderly couple. Abraham and Sarah, both of them well on the wrong side of youth. Sarah was unable to have children, and at their age there was no chance of a family in any case. Then one day, we hear, God told Abraham to leave his home and go to an unspecified destination in a distant land where he would become the father of more children than there were stars in the sky. Whatever we make of this story, there are strands running through it that might speak to us today. First, these old people, more than ready perhaps for peaceful retirement, are told to up sticks and leave everything they knew and make a journey to an unknown land. Then they are told they will have not just one unlikely baby, but a whole new nation of offspring.

Could such a story unfold in our lives? Could a fable from long ago be relevant to the lives of twenty-first-century elders? Leave what you know, take the risk of journeying into the unknown, and your lives will bear more fruit than you can imagine. This is a supreme challenge to faith, however we think of 'faith'. As elders, with our long memory of how the world is, can we – dare we – allow hope to overrule despair? Faith, expressed like this, could tip the scales of our troubled world away from the edge of the abyss and towards a horizon where the dawn of a new beginning defies all the darkness of the night,

Like Abraham and Sarah, we probably think our race is almost run, and there is nothing left for us to do. Their story is a startling wake-up call, announcing that our declining years are potentially the most fruitful of all the seasons of our lives if we are willing to grow beyond our habitual comfort zones and set out towards the beckoning horizon. This call urges us to see those later big birthdays as invitations to embark on a new adventure – the sacred adventure into wisdom. The journey that calls us onward isn't a demand to emigrate to the other side of the world. It's an inner journey, not drawing us further away from those we love, but with the power to draw us closer.

I love this story, which like all stories is probably not meant to be taken literally. Its deeper meaning urges me to live adventurously, to trust in the possibility enclosed in the heart of the apparently impossible. The impossible becomes possible when we make our daily journey, choice by choice, believing that it can be so.

It matters how we respond to the challenge of living the bigger picture. Our future may actually depend on it, as the story of the puddlefish reminds us …

There was once a big tree growing beside a river. Every year after the wet season, a puddle would be left behind in the hollow formed by the tree's roots. And every year a small school of puddle-fish would settle in this puddle. There they spent all their time swimming in circles, trying to catch water-bugs, and fighting over what they caught.

Then one day there was a huge splash, and a brightly coloured rainbow-fish flopped into the puddle, after leaping out of the river below.

The puddle-fish, shocked by this new arrival, all huddled at the side of the pool and waited, carefully observing the newcomer. The big fish seemed to glow with iridescence, and he was smiling.

One bold puddle-fish made a move towards him. 'Who are you? Where are you from?'

'I come from the ocean,' came the reply.

'What is "ocean"?' the puddle-fish asked.

'Well,' said the rainbow fish, 'ocean is … ocean

is … it's what we're made for. It goes on for ever. It's full of so many wonderful creatures. It's brimming with movement and life.'

'How do you get there?' asked the puddle-fish, eager to discover this new wonder. 'You just jump out of the puddle, and trust the river to carry you there,' the rainbow-fish assured him.

But then the objections started to rise up from the ranks of the puddle-fish.

The realist-fish objected: 'This puddle is reality. You are deluded about the ocean.'

The scaredy-fish whimpered: 'No one would ever dare make that leap into the great unknown.'

The political-fish proposed: 'Both sides of the argument have merit. We should form a discussion group and talk it through.'

'Talking won't get you to the ocean,' the rainbow fish warned them gently. 'And summer is coming. Soon this little puddle will dry up, and then what?'

Eventually the visiting fish leapt back into the river and swam away.

And, very tentatively, a few brave puddle-fish also took the leap of faith. The others gazed after them with pity, and went back to swimming round in circles, hunting for water-bugs, and fighting over what they caught.

As we grow in wisdom, learning continually from our experience and reflecting on what it teaches us, we arrive at the point of choosing. Will we stay in the puddle until it dries up, or will we trust the messenger from the ocean and take the leap of faith into a future we can't imagine, but are invited to trust?

If we can learn to live adventurously, we may find that the gap narrows between where we are and where we would like to be, or even how the world is and how we would like the world to be, and what seemed impossible becomes possible. Christopher Reeve assures us in these words:

> *So many of our dreams at first seem impossible, then they seem improbable, and then when we summon the will, they soon become inevitable.*

Living adventurously is the terrain of the mystic, who sees just a little bit further than the current horizon. The mystic is the carrier of the vision that the world needs perhaps more urgently than any other gift.

PAUSE FOR THOUGHT

- How would you define the role of mystic? And the role of 'prophet'? Do you feel yourself drawn to engage with your own inner mystic and inner prophet?
- Can you identify with the boundary geese? Maybe you are feeling isolated as friends pass away, or you have had to leave familiar places where you may have lived for many years. You feel, and you are, vulnerable – susceptible to illness or physical frailty. Yet you probably do more than you realise to 'protect the breeding flock'.
- How do you warn the flock if you think it is heading in a wrong direction? How do you help the young discern the values to guide their lives?

- What is your own inner mystic seeing in the future vision of what the human family can become?
- To what potential dangers is your inner prophet alerting you? How do you feel about flying on the edge?
- As you reflect back over just the past few days or weeks, when do you feel you were living cautiously, and when were you living adventurously? How do you feel about your choices?

CHAPTER 8

WHEN THE SEED DIES

~

When I return to forever, may the circle be closed and the spiral broader.
Marlo Morgan

SURELY THE GREATEST adventure of our lives will be the leap into the unknown that we call death – the moment when we arrive at the brink of our physical existence on earth and, like the timorous, curious, adventurous puddle-fish we have to face the leap from our little, finite puddle into the flowing river.

A very powerful influence on our later years is, for most of us, the growing awareness of our own mortality and the inevitability of this leap into apparent oblivion. Indeed, when I ask close friends whether death is something they think about, they tell me that thoughts of their own physical ending are never far away. This isn't, I suggest, a morbid pre-occupation, but a healthy curiosity, along with some understandable apprehension, about what, if anything, may await us at the moment of our passing and beyond it. What does Wisdom ask of us, in the face of these existential questions? Can it help us navigate these potentially troubling waters?

In our western culture especially, death is not a comfortable topic. On the contrary, it is almost a social taboo, sanitised in funeral homes and distanced from daily life. Other cultures are less inhibited in their exploration of the natural process of dying. Death is not easy to deal with, but impossible to avoid. Friends may have died already and when our parents die we become the front line generation. As a friend once wryly observed: 'God is fishing at our end of the pond now'.

Wisdom prompts us to reflect on a few important questions:

- How will I prepare for my own departure?

- How do I feel about it?
- What do I think comes next, if anything?

PREPARING FOR DEATH

Most of us want to make things easier for those who come after us, but most of us are also prone to procrastination, reluctant to face the inevitable approach of the unavoidable. There are probably millions of homes with loft space and cellars and garages crammed with the relics of the ages, often going back over several generations of those whose belongings we have inherited and now don't know what to do with. Anyone who has had the difficult task of clearing a house after the death of a family member will understand too well that the process involves both backache and heartache, as we sift through items that once meant a great deal to their owners and now trigger memories and possibly tears.

How do we set about this task of easing the pain for those who will have to tidy up after us?

We should begin by recognising that our choice of lifestyle needs to partner with consideration for the next generation. It's easy, and lazy, to settle into the comfort zone of our familiar and cluttered home and regard the future, perhaps unconsciously, as 'someone else's problem'. But do we really intend to transfer the problem to our children?

If not then there will probably be a need to do some serious de-cluttering and embrace a simpler lifestyle. What is stopping us? What are we still clinging to? Certainly this task is a painful one. A simple approach might be to take stock of our belongings, maybe room by room and gently over time, sort what we find into three piles, asking ourselves:

- Do I still use this item? Does it hold memories I'm not yet ready to part with? Does it still bring me joy? This pile is for keeping
- Has this item outlived its usefulness? I haven't used it/worn it/read it for several years (or ever) but it's still in reasonable condition. This pile is for items that might be sold, or donated to the charity shop or the next jumble sale.
- Has this item gone beyond its useful life? Is it time to let it go to the recycling centre?

Wisdom urges us to do this necessary work now, while we are still able. If we don't, someone else, who doesn't have the time because they are working and raising their own family, will 'inherit' it. This is not Wisdom's way.

This practical process can also be a spiritual exercise, inviting us to sift through the accumulations of our years. Perhaps you can recall times when you have been re-decorating, and spent more time with the old newspapers spread out to catch the paint drips than with the paint and brushes? The old newspapers took you right back, evoking memories, maybe laughter too, or tears. Clearing up your life is also an opportunity for sifting – letting the memories slip gently through your fingers without regrets or recriminations, reflecting on what has been life-giving and what has not, cherishing the former and letting the latter go.

Preparing ourselves emotionally and spiritually for our departure is another matter altogether, and will depend very much on how we feel about our mortality …

OUR ATTITUDE TO DEATH

Over the past few months I have been privileged to witness several different approaches to death, as various friends have made their final crossing. Of course, everyone is unique and will approach death in a unique way, but I have learned something from each of these people.

One friend received a terminal diagnosis with great dignity and positivity. His first words were that he would now be devoting himself to what he called 'the serious business of dying'. He worked on this sacred project for nine months, and the parallel to the months of pregnancy was not lost on us. He was a very tall man – we used to call him a hazard to low-flying aircraft – and would have been the first to admit to having a well-developed ego. During the nine months of his dying, he shrank physically, as one might expect, but spiritually he grew almost visibly. His true self grew as his ego-self shrank.

A second friend had almost no time to adjust to the imminence of death. From diagnosis to death took just seven days, during which he focused not on his own ending and considerable suffering, but on his friends. He used his remaining strength to contact us, share memories and thank us for the gift of our friendship. He faced his death with dignity and courage, with no trace of self-pity or bitterness.

Not everyone is able to bring such qualities to their final journey. Disease and distress rob many of us of this option. A third friend fought against his dying all the way, and experienced a great deal of agitation and inner torment. This was partly due to the toxins building in his failing body, and the powerful medication affecting his mind. He made the final journey in a haze of self-focused anger and fear and burdened by a great deal of unfinished business.

And finally, sadly, there was the friend (in a different country) whose pain was being well managed by good palliative care but who felt unable to contemplate the end and thus chose to bring it forward by finding a doctor to collude in an act of assisted dying.

I learned something from all four of these friends – from one the gift of acceptance and the proactive letting go of lesser concerns to focus on what matters most – from another the courage in facing a sudden and painful death while reaching out to friends and loved ones in gratitude and love – from a third the importance of attending to unfinished business while there is still time. And from the fourth? The hope that I might find the courage, when the time comes, to stay the course, the humility to acknowledge that I might not, and compassion for all, whatever their decision in extremity. None of us should presume to make judgements over how others face their dying, and none of us knows how we ourselves will respond to the final days.

How do we actually view our death? It can be more helpful, and perhaps more deeply true, to regard death not as finality, but as *mystery*.

Finality closes a door on all we are. Mystery opens a door to the possibility of transformation in ways beyond our human understanding.

Shakespeare captures something of the mystery of transformation in *The Tempest*. The ethereal Ariel consoles Ferdinand, whose father is presumed to have drowned in a shipwreck, with these words:

Full fathom five thy father lies.
Of his bones are coral made.
Those are pearls that were his eyes.
Nothing of him that doth fade
But doth suffer a sea change
Into something rich and strange.

What kind of 'sea change' might our bodily dying open up? Shakespeare hopes for 'something rich and strange', in other words, something infinitely more than we can imagine and utterly different from anything we have known. Mystery. Not finality.

Unfortunately, and unhelpfully, some religious teaching has encouraged us to believe in a post-mortem future not as something 'rich' but a very conditional reward granted only to those who have kept all the (man-made) rules on earth, and not as something 'strange' but an unending continuation of life more or less as we know it, but stripped of all unpleasantness.

Christian scripture has wiser thoughts on the matter, offering, for example, the analogy of the seed that, as long as it remains just a single seed, will never bear fruit, but if it falls into the ground, disintegrates and rots, it will bring forth new life in abundance. (John 12:24)

DOES MY LIFE AMOUNT TO ANYTHING?

Another analogy from Judaic scripture paints a beautiful picture of how the rain and the snow fall from heaven and do not return without giving life-giving water to the earth, making seeds sprout and plants grow (Isaiah 55:10).

Yet many are plagued in their dying months by the anxiety that their lives have not amounted to anything. One friend of mine, in particular, whose life and work had, quite literally, changed hundreds of thousands of lives, asked me this question as he was dying. He couldn't believe that his 'raindrop' had caused so many good seeds to germinate before it returned to 'heaven'.

Another dear friend whose life had been devoted to others - family, friends and community - in outstanding ways, commented to me as he was dying that it was a terrible thing to end life as you began, helpless and dependent, having, as it were 'come full circle' back to infancy, with nothing to show for it.

For me, knowing him as I did, it was obvious that the trajectory of his life (and surely of all our lives) was not a circle but a *spiral.* I could see so clearly in my friend's life, as he could not, how the way he had lived his life had formed a spiral, raising him in small, everyday ways, closer and closer to the best he could be, and, in some mysterious way, encouraging and helping all of us to rise closer to our 'best', our most fully human.

Our lives are not a circle, but a spiral. Every choice we make, every conversation, every gesture, every interaction will either raise the spiral of our lives a little, or bring it down a little. The life-giving, love-motivated choices will raise our spiral . The destructive, ego-dominated choices will tend to pull it downwards. Love, in its truest form of choosing in every situation to do the more loving thing (however we might be feeling), determines whether the 'raindrop' of our brief lives on earth returns to its origins having added to the store of love, life and hope in the world, or diminished it.

IS THERE ANYTHING OUT THERE?

Most of us will, from time to time, pause to wonder what, if anything, lies beyond the horizon of our earthly lives. In human terms there is no answer to this perennial question, and it might be wise to distrust those who presume to describe the nature of that 'beyond', or even offer us guaranteed ways of achieving immortality. Mortality is, whether we accept it or not, an incontrovertible fact of our earthly, physical existence.

We do know, however, from basic school science, that life as we know it involves both matter and energy. Matter dies with us, and returns to earth, through burial or cremation. But what of 'energy'? Science tells us that energy cannot be either created or destroyed, but only transmitted and transformed. When I ponder these things, I become more and more convinced that the energy that first animated our bodies at conception and leaves them on death, must also be governed by this scientific principle. This brings us right back to the possibility of transformation – that the energy that drove and defined us in life can take a different form beyond the horizon of our understanding. Most spiritual traditions honour and nourish this possibility, and the best of them stop short of trying to explain it or describe it.

Two incidents in my own life come to mind as I explore these matters.

The first happened just after the former East and

West Germany were reunited in 1990, after their enforced post-war separation. I had lived for three years in West Berlin during the years of separation, when the Cold War was at its height. Back then West Berlin was a political island in the middle of communist East Germany. It was a city severed from its hinterland. Its street names reflected the places those streets had once led to – Potsdamerstraße for example, would once have led to the now inaccessible Potsdam. The names of bridges reflected the names of the communities they once connected, and now divided. Every underground line and bus route that would once have brought you to a destination now definitively out of bounds, ended with the conductor's instruction 'End of the line. Everyone disembark.'

As a recently arrived resident in Berlin I had never known any of these places, but when I visited Berlin again after reunification, and made a road trip up to the Baltic coast, I was like a child in a candy store, recognising the real places that had once been just street signs and discovering living communities all with their own personalities and characteristics. The street signs that had defined and limited my own years living in the city had been always pointing beyond themselves to a reality beyond my experience.

This memory seems to me to be a potent metaphor for how so much in our earthly lives is also a pointer to something beyond itself, a different kind of reality that we cannot begin to imagine … Until, perhaps, on the other side of the mystery, we become part of it.

The second incident happened while I was at a retreat centre in Chicago. At the end of the retreat a bonfire was lit in the courtyard and we were invited to sit around it and reflect on our own lives. Eventually the

fire burned down, and it seemed as though the dying sparks of the fire were taking flight and lighting up the night sky. This display was actually the appearance of clouds and clouds of fireflies – something I had never seen in my own part of the world, but for me it felt like an image of a new form of energy emerging from the dying embers and carrying life far beyond itself – like a thousand new stars being flung into space in the wake of a supernova explosion, new beginnings from a traumatic ending.

Perhaps a large part of our fear of death is a fear of separation. Children experience separation anxiety when their prime carer(s) go(es) temporarily out of sight. They grow out of it when they learn that a person doesn't cease to exist just because we can't see them. Might this feel true in the face of physical death? We are a bit like the spokes of a wheel. When we look out into space we feel terrified of our aloneness, but if we focus back to the hub, we realise we belong to something much greater, from which we are never truly separated.

We can change these perceptions. We can look out beyond the horizon and trust in the wonder it contains as well as recognising the existential fear it may evoke. We can acknowledge that we are at once both *alone* and *all-one* in this mystery of life, in some ways isolated in our present limited consciousness, but also inseparably connected to a much greater whole.

THE RIVER OF LIFE FLOWS ON

As I move into the final chapter of my own life, I wonder about the metaphors we use to capture our feelings about the shape and meaning of the life we have lived. Is it something like a highway with a beginning, an end and a purpose, a journey with a start line and a destination? Or is it more like a circle with no beginning or ending, but only change and transformation from one form to another. More like the circulation of our bloodstream or the flow of a river to the ocean and then back to the clouds, to fall again in a new form.

A highway can be engineered, to take the best route towards its desired destination. It is imagined as being under human control, primarily serving human purposes. In many ways our lives can be seen through this lens.

The river never ends but changes form, from water to steam through evaporation, and back to water again in a different place, through condensation. It is suggestive of life as a continuous flow through space and time. Flowing water brings life wherever it flows. It follows the contours of the land and at the same time shapes and re-shapes those contours. Our lives too are shaped by the situations into which we are born, just as they also shape those situations, for good or ill.

Both these images of life have merit. Life as a journey with a beginning and an end reminds us that we are on our way to something more – a destination that we could call 'the best we can be', both individually and collectively. It lends purpose and meaning to our understanding of ourselves and our destiny.

Life as a meandering river reminds us that we are part of an apparently infinite continuum, and that our own personal life will reach a point in time at which we will have no choice but to surrender it to a mystery we cannot understand.

At the end of our lives we may well reflect on how we have impacted the world, and whether we are leaving it in a better state than it was when we were born. What destination has our personal highway arrived at? But the bigger picture tells us the ending is a continuance in a different form. Both are valid and valuable, yet in the end it is the river metaphor that calls us forward. Our limited destination becomes just a staging post on a far greater journey being made by all life.

But the stream has its own story of living and dying …

High in the far-off mountains, a little stream sprang from its hidden source. It flowed down the mountainside, through all kinds of different terrain, sometimes leaping and bubbling, sometimes drifting lazily or going underground, but it was never stopped by any obstacle that might have got in its way.

One day, it reached the edge of a vast desert. 'Just one more obstacle to overcome,' it thought to itself. 'Nothing has ever stopped me flowing, and I shall surely overcome this obstacle too.' And so the stream flung itself at the desert. But each time it did so, its waters simply disappeared, trickling away into nothingness, swallowed up by the dry, hot sand.

But the stream was not to be deterred. If its destiny was to cross this desert, then it would surely find a way. 'If the wind can cross the desert, so can the stream,' it thought to itself, and the desert seemed to echo back these words: 'The winds cross the desert and so can the stream.'

And so began a conversation between the stream and the desert sand. 'I know I must cross this desert,' the stream told the sand, 'but every time I try, the sand swallows me up. No matter how hard I fling myself at the desert, I don't get any further.

The desert replied, 'You won't be able to cross the desert using the same methods that worked for you further up the mountain. It's no use hurling yourself at the desert like that. You will never cross the sand like this. You will simply disappear, or turn into marshland. No, you must trust the wind to carry you across the desert. You must let yourself be carried,'

'How can the wind carry me across the desert?' the stream asked in disbelief.

'You must let yourself be absorbed into the wind, and then the wind will carry you,' the desert replied.

But the stream didn't like this idea. After all, it was a stream, with a nature and identity of its own.

It didn't at all want to lose itself by being absorbed into the wind. The desert sensed the stream's fears, and tried to offer reassurance.

'That's what the wind does,' it told the stream. 'Trust me, and trust the wind. If you let yourself be absorbed by the wind, it will carry you across the desert and let you fall again on the other side, to be a stream again.'

The stream wasn't convinced. 'But I won't be the same stream that I am now. I won't be this particular stream.'

The desert understood this dilemma, but the desert also understood the mystery: 'You certainly won't be the same stream you are now if you fling yourself into the sand and turn into a marsh. But let the wind carry you across the desert, and the real heart of you, the essence of who you truly are, will be born again on the other side, to flow a new course, to be a river that you can't even imagine from where you are standing now.'

The stream thought for a while, and something deep in its heart had a memory of a wind that could be trusted, and a horizon that was always out of reach, but was always a new beginning. So the stream took a deep breath, and surrendered to the power of the wind.

The hot desert wind transformed the stream into vapour, then raised up the vapour and carried it in strong and loving arms far beyond the horizon, high above the hot desert sand, and let it fall again softly at the top of a new mountain, far away. And the stream began to understand who it really was, and what it meant to be a stream.

DEPARTING IN PEACE

At the end of our lives we stand on the edge of a mystery that we cannot understand or cross in our own strength. We fear the loss of our identity, lacking understanding of the power of transformation, and resistant to the call to yield to the energy of the Spirit.

Christian scripture tells the story of how an old man, Simeon, encountered the infant Jesus. It evokes a beautiful image of a very old man, about to depart, holding a newborn child in his arms. Simeon is all our grandfathers and his prayer in this sacred moment has become enshrined in Christian liturgy as the Nunc Dimittis. A wise man, about to cross the horizon of death welcomes the child about to embark on the adventure of earthly life. He prays to the Holy One 'Now let your servant depart in peace, for I have seen with my own eyes, in my own life, the presence and the power of the Holy.'

This moment assures us, if we have eyes to see, that death is not a fracturing but a completion of the circle of life

PAUSE FOR THOUGHT

- How ready do you feel to prepare for your own dying, both practically and spiritually? Is anything asking for your attention?

- How do you feel about returning to childhood dependency as your physical needs increase?

- Does the image of the spiral give you a different perspective

- Who do you know whose life has been an upward spiral?
- Can you believe yours can be too?
- What are your own feelings about 'life after death'?
- How does the story of The Stream speak to you?
- Simeon prays: 'Now let your servant depart in peace for my eyes have seen the Mystery'. It reminds us that we too have known the presence of the Holy in our lives. Can you make your own departure prayer like this?

CHAPTER 9

OUR LEGACY TO THE FUTURE

We do not inherit the Earth from our Ancestors.
We borrow it from our Children.
Native American proverb

WE MAY FEEL like an isolated minority, somewhat side-lined from mainstream society, and this can cause us to lose sight of the reality that we are, of course, part of a long generational continuum of life. We can also easily forget that, just as we stand on giants' shoulders, so we are becoming the next layer of growth of that same giant, and soon the next generation will be standing on *our* shoulders, whether they realise it or not.

Every generation builds on the wisdom and experience of those who have gone before. We all benefit from the inventiveness, creativity, courage and generosity of our ancestors. So the fruits of our own lives will add to that human mountain, and our descendants will be able to climb even higher and see even further into the distant land beyond our own horizon.

What can we give them along their way into the future? What might our legacy be to that still unseen future? Johann Wolfgang von Goethe suggests that 'children only need two things from their parents: roots and wings'. This is a good summary of what 'legacy' means in this context. Our own lives add to the strength and health of the *roots* of humanity by passing on the best of human values to those who come after us, and by giving them *wings,* to fly the next part of the journey in their own way.

As elders we play a crucial and unique role in this process of passing on the fruits of our own lives to those who follow after us. But this isn't as easy as it sounds.

The Christian tradition records a parable told by Jesus that has much to tell us about this problem. He warns his listeners not to try to mend a garment by sewing a patch of new cloth onto it, because the new cloth will shrink and put a strain on the old, causing the patch to tear away from the garment, making the damage even worse (Matthew 9:16-17). He goes on to give a similar warning about not putting new wine into old wineskins because the new wine will cause the old skins to burst, and both the wine and the wineskins will be lost.

Both these metaphors resonate with the tension between the generations when the old try to impose their ways on the young: the young may become 'tearaways' and 'burst out of' attitudes that they feel are stifling them. In our own times we express a similar warning in the phrase 'you can't put an old head on young shoulders. This is more than a warning. It is statement of reality.

So in offering the fruits of our lives we face two big

challenges: first, to pass on whatever guidance we can, while at the same time allowing the next generation to find its own way forward. But, as already on this journey, the butterflies can help us....

INTER-GENERATIONAL CO-OPERATION

Some butterflies make migratory journeys of thousands of miles, for example from Mexico to Canada and back.

A butterfly typically weighs less than a gram, and only has a short life span. If you work out how far a butterfly can fly in one lifetime and how far it is from Mexico to Canada, you'll realise that it's an impossible feat for a single butterfly.

It becomes possible when they fly in relays.

It takes up to four generations to complete the distance, flying in stages and resting at known places *en route*, where they go through the whole process from mating to metamorphosis, until the next generation is ready to make the next leg of the journey.

When we reflect on this multi-generational approach to the journey two things become apparent:

- The next generation has to fly the *next* stage of the journey, not the previous stage. If the adult butterflies were to say: 'Fly exactly where I flew', then there would be no progress at all. Each generation has to live life as they find it, with the particular joys and hazards along the way – that the parent generation could not have foreseen or prepared them for.

- There is some intuitive knowledge in the species that 'knows the way' and recognises landmarks that they themselves have never seen. We could call this 'the wisdom of the way', and this is something that we, the elders, can and must pass on to our young, in whatever way we can.

PROVIDING THE ROOTS

We can't give the next generation a roadmap for their onward journey because the map we used ourselves doesn't cover their future terrain. What we *can* pass on is the *values* that we feel have guided us along the way – bearing in mind that 'values' are not the same as creeds and doctrines. Values are best passed on by living them ourselves in ways made visible in our behaviour towards others and the way we make our choices.

These values that have guided us and previous generations and helped us navigate a true course through life's twisting pathways are the *roots* that will also nourish those who follow after, and hold them steady in life's storms.

Just as we struggle to digest the ways of the younger generation, so too we can't simply transplant our wisdom into their lives or expect them to digest our ways. We can't tell others how to live their lives, but we can show them how we live our own lives. The way in which we respond to life situations and the attitudes we display will have more influence than anything we say.

I was once leading a retreat for a large group of religious sisters. We had been reflecting on the story of Noah and the flood, and on what went into the ark. The story itself describes a catastrophic natural disaster (probably an ancient memory of a tsunami) and what you would need in order to make a new beginning after a traumatic breakdown. Thus, the breeding pairs of the animals would be the seed corns for a new start to life. I invited the sisters to reflect on what aspects of their faith, or sense of the Holy, would be most essential, in their view, to pass on to the next generation. We then all took some time in silence to ponder this question.

I must admit that I had expected these women, whose lives were committed to a lifestyle in conformance with the teachings of a traditional church institution, to suggest aspects of doctrine and practice, Bible reading, catechism, and attendance at church that the young would need to observe, but to my surprise what they brought back from their reflection centred entirely around the nature of the Holy, as they perceived it. They proposed that it would be supremely important to pass on:

- The generosity …
- The compassion …
- The patience …
- The gentleness …
- The peace …
- The justice …
- The kindness …
- The joy …
- The faithfulness of the Holy.

I had mistakenly expected them to identify things one should teach the young *about* the Holy and things one should do to acquire this knowledge and keep it alive. Instead they identified aspects of the holy that we *experience* in our real lives, and would want the next generation to come to experience for themselves.

I listened attentively and then I asked myself: how would you pass on these attributes? And I realised with a shock: we don't pass on these values by talking about them, writing about them, preaching them. We pass them on by living them – by incarnating them in our own lives. We pass on the patience of God, for example, by being patient ourselves.

It is so simple. And it is extremely challenging. Far easier to talk about it all, but so difficult to make it incarnate in our own daily lives.

I heard a story about how divine compassion can be made incarnate, when a young curate, recently arrived in an urban parish, shared his experience of being called to a bereaved family one night. Their baby had died, and the bereaved mother had called the parish priest for support, but the parish priest wasn't at home, and the curate had to attend.

When he arrived at the house the baby's father opened the door, and was obviously not pleased to see him. 'Your wife called me,' explained the curate and reluctantly the husband let him in. Once inside, and finding himself surrounded by devastated family members mourning the loss of this little baby the curate had no idea what to say. All he could do was stand and weep with the family.

A few weeks later the curate was surprised to be approached by the father, as he was walking down the street. 'I just want to thank you for coming to us when our baby died,' he said. 'I guess you could tell that I didn't want you there. To be honest, if you had said anything pious, like "God wanted another little angel for heaven" I would have smashed your face in. But you stood there and wept with us. And I thank you for that. It meant so much.'

The curate's tears were worth a thousand sermons. The compassion of God had been expressed and made real in the midst of a family's grief, and no words were spoken.

ENABLING THE WINGS

Our wings get clipped in many ways as we go through life. We feel inadequate, perhaps because we have been discouraged by apparent failures, or overloaded with destructive criticism. What can we learn from our own experience about how to enable the wings of the young so that they trust themselves to fly their own course into the future?

I remember once being in rather a low place in my life, feeling that I was not doing anything very useful, including not being very good, I felt, at my new role as a grandmother. My son-in-law picked up on this low mood and asked me how I was feeling. This in itself was a boost to my drooping wings. With some hesitation I shared with him that I was very conscious that he and my daughter (both medics) were out saving lives every day of the week, and that my own contribution to the human race seemed very poor by comparison. Also that I didn't rate my performance as a grandmother very highly either.

He listened attentively, until I turned to leave. Then he called me back. 'Margaret', he said, 'There's something you need to hear.' My heart sank. What had I done, or failed to do? Having spent much of my earlier life with people who were overly negative, I had come to expect criticism as a first response to most things. I stopped in my tracks, fearful of what might be coming. Then he said this to me: 'You're right. We do go out every day and save lives. It's our job. But what,' he asked me, 'is the point in saving lives if people have no vision to live for?'

Suddenly, through his eyes, I could see that what I was doing was worth something. That morning he gave me wings.

We may well wonder how we can help others to find their wings. Some suggestions:

- Encouraging them, with genuine positivity drawn from our own experience of having been encouraged
- Holding back on advice and criticism. It's worth asking 'Is this helpful?' before offering any advice
- Listening with genuine respect to their opinions and thoughts
- Letting them make their own mistakes, just as we did ourselves, because mistakes are the best teachers
- Recognising the power of youthful imagination and creativity
- Avoiding, like the plague, any hint of an 'I know better' attitude
- Not helping too much. When we take over a task, it's tantamount to saying that they are incapable of doing it themselves. Too much help impedes their growth and learning and becomes a hindrance
- Being open to learning from them and letting them see that this is happening.

It was in a hospital ward that I was given the most surprising and beautiful insight into the secret of giving the gift of roots and wings. My (then fifteen-year-old) granddaughter and I had been visiting a relative who was dying. She's not a girl who wears her heart on her sleeve, but 'still waters run deep'. Occasionally she comes out with comments that astound me. This was one such occasion. I asked her how she was feeling in the face of this imminent loss. She was very quiet for a few moments and then looked me in the eye and said how devastated she would be if it were me who was about to leave this life. I was honestly shocked at the depth of feeling she was expressing. I wondered, perhaps out loud in some form, what I had ever done to warrant such powerful feeling on her part. Then she said this: 'Grandma, it's nothing to do with anything you've said, or done. It's about your *presence*.'

At that moment I recognised a bond between us that didn't depend on any words or actions of mine. What she valued was quite simply that I was there, in her life, quietly and unconditionally. Loving presence is a gift we can give even, and perhaps especially, when we feel helpless to do or say anything. It goes deeper than words and it transcends time and distance. Being lovingly present to another person happens when 'heart speaks to heart' and the heart has a language of its own, best heard in the silence that remains when our own words fail.

A traditional story describes rather beautifully how a wise and understanding teacher provides a child with roots, by incarnating the kindness, gentleness and love of the Holy, and enables that child to discover her wings and fly into the future with new confidence ...

Little Maria was born with a cleft palate. She lived in a poor country and there were no doctors nearby to help her. So she grew up with a very distorted face, unable to drink properly or even to smile. The other children made fun of her, and even many of the grown-ups seemed uncomfortable around her. She felt very lonely and unloved.

But one day a new teacher arrived at the village school. She was so pretty and so kind, and all the children wanted to please her. But Maria stayed back, out of sight as far as possible, afraid that this teacher too would not want to be near her.

Time passed, and the new teacher seemed to be at ease with everyone, including Maria, yet Maria found it hard to trust. She remained defensive and withdrawn. Until one day when the teacher asked the children to write a story about themselves.

Maria didn't know what to write. The story of her life was not a nice one. But perhaps she could make it into a better story. So at the end of class she handed in a different story, that went like this. 'There was once a little girl who was born ugly, and no one would play with her. But one day an angel came to visit her as she slept. The angel bent over the little girl, so lovingly, and kissed her brow. And when she woke the next morning the little girl looked in the mirror, and saw that she was beautiful. The angel's kiss had transformed her overnight and she lived happily ever after.'

That night the teacher read the stories the children had written. And as she read Maria's story, a tear fell from her eyes. The next day she handed the stories back to the children, and Maria took her story back, expecting a bad mark. But instead she found this message written at the bottom of the page: 'Maria, I wish you were my little girl,' the teacher had written. But the words were a bit smudged, where the teacher's tear had fallen.

And from that day onwards, Maria knew that her dream had come true, and an angel really had kissed her, and she would never be the same again. She had discovered her wings.

CROSS-GENERATIONAL JUSTICE

As elders in a rapidly changing society we often look back and think how massively different today's world is from the one in which we grew up. Probably every generation feels this, but it really does seem as though the pace of change has become faster and fiercer in the past few decades, and not all the change has been for the good.

As a child born just before the end of World War II, I inherited a world just emerging from deadly conflict and cherishing the hope of global peace. While this universal hope has not been fulfilled, at least in my own native land we have not been faced with any existential threat on our own shores. I had come to assume that my whole life would be lived in a context of (at least local) peace. Until recently ... when a newly aroused, and still perilously underestimated, shadow of nationalism, international acts of unprovoked aggression, a few dangerous ego-driven demagogues and frighteningly invasive technology has darkened the face of the world.

As I grew up I had the benefit of world-class health care, free at the point of need, and excellent, free education opportunities. When my generation left school we moved on to free higher education, and good job prospects, which in turn opened up the possibility of entry into the housing market. Now, in the last chapter of our lives, we enjoy the relative security of retirement pensions ...

And now? Our young people are growing up under ever-darkening clouds of potential global conflict, climate breakdown and the still-unknown threats inherent in the advance of artificial intelligence. They are living through a serious cost of living crisis, soaring costs of housing, higher education and the ordinary needs of daily life. Many are continuing to live with parents, unable to break into the housing market or afford the ever-rising rental costs and risks. Their job prospects are limited and childcare impossibly expensive. They face the erosion of our cherished free health care and their chances of a state-funded pension in their retirement are slender

This amounts to serious cross-generational injustice, and many elders want to do what they can to mitigate the hardships for the younger generation. The Bank of Mum and Dad, we learn, is now the biggest lender of funds to support home purchase and higher education costs, and older relatives and friends the biggest providers of childcare.

How do you feel about this unjust situation that none of us ordinary mortals has caused or deserved? How might we, the elders help to level out the hardships?

YOUR PERSONAL LEGACY

How would you want to be remembered? One way to approach this question is to have a go at writing your own obituary. Don't take on this task with too heavy a heart – just reflect on what you would wish people might say or think about you when you are gone. It is for your eyes only so feel free to express your highest hopes. I learned something important once when I mentioned this exercise in my own family circle and the following suggestion came out (amid kindly laughter): 'She wrote a lot of nonsense, but we loved her!' I realised at once how much I would prefer this to the alternative 'She wrote world-class masterpieces, but we couldn't stand the woman!' Even a lighted-hearted response like this makes you realise instantly that you would much rather be loved than admired, much rather be embraced in a family hug than put on a pedestal.

Once you begin to notice which qualities in your own life you value most and would wish to be remembered for, you can start to nourish these qualities actively and intentionally in your daily life – a bit like polishing your spiritual silver so as to pass it on at its very best to those you love and who will follow after you.

Another traditional tale teaches similar wisdom about the most important human values and gives us a clue about what true leadership would look like…

Once there was a Native American chief who was nearing the end of his life. Even though he had tried many times, he was not able to decide which of his sons should succeed him as chief.

One day, he gathered his sons together and told

them, 'Do you see that mountain in the distance? I want you to journey to that mountain, climb to its summit and bring back the thing you think will be most helpful in leading our people in the future.'

After several days the first son returned with some flint stones used to make arrow tips and spear points. He told his father, 'Our people will never live in fear of their enemies. I know where there are large stocks of flint.'

The second son climbed to the top of the mountain, and on the way found forests rich with wood for making fires. When he returned, he said to his father, 'Our people will never be cold in winter. I know where wood can be found in abundance to keep them warm and to cook their food.'

The third son returned late and empty-handed. He told his story: 'On my way to the summit I passed much that would be very useful for our people, but something made me keep on walking. The summit was barren rock, but then I looked further towards the horizon, far into the distance. I was astonished to see new land filled with forests and meadows, mountains and valleys, fish and animals – a land of great beauty and great peace. I brought nothing back, for the land was still far off and I didn't have time to travel there, but I would love to go there some day; I delayed coming back because I found it very difficult to return after seeing the beauty and the promise of that land.'

The old chief's eyes blazed. He grasped his third son in his arms, proclaiming that he would succeed him as the new chief. He thought to himself, 'My other sons brought back worthy, necessary things. But my third son has a vision. He has seen a better land, the promised land, and he burns with the desire to go there.'

What is *your* personal vision for the future of humanity?

Whatever your vision, it probably hovers over a distant horizon that seems far away and out of reach. Don't let this dismay or discourage you.

There was once a young man who applied for a job as a long distance truck driver in Canada. On his first day he was told that he would be driving the route from Montreal in the east to Vancouver in the west of the country, mainly at night, over at least three or four nights. He climbed into the driver's cab and turned on the ignition and the lights. The light beam, he noted, reached only about five metres into the dark night. 'I am about to embark on a journey of three thousand kilometres,' he thought to himself, 'and my lights only reach for a few metres into the darkness'.

So what did he do next? Perhaps he dismissed the challenge as impossible, switched off the ignition and went off to look for a more manageable job. Or perhaps he started to drive, and discovered that the light travelled with him.

Navigating the juggernaut of older age through the maze of modern life, carrying the cargo of your accumulated knowledge and experience of the ways of human beings and your store of mainly unacknowledged wisdom, you may sometimes feel that you can't go on. At moments like these, remember the truck driver, and stay with the journey. The light will travel with you.

Christian scripture asserts that 'the light shines in the darkness and the darkness cannot overcome it.' At one level this is obvious. Try opening your door on a dark night in winter. Does the darkness come into your house? Or does the light in your house stream out into the darkness?

Something similar could be said about your legacy to the future. The light of life was ignited in you at the moment of your conception. It has travelled with you all along, albeit only illuminating the next few steps.

But it has done more than this: it has been magnified through every loving, life-giving choice you have made and has become a light shared with others, helping to guide their journeys too. They have recognised this light in you through your loving presence, though you may never have been aware yourself of the power of this presence.

What then, when you are no longer physically present? Loving presence, surely, is like the light that shines in the darkness that the darkness cannot extinguish. Your absence, even your apparently final absence in death, cannot and will not extinguish the loving energy your presence has given to the world – energy that can be neither created nor destroyed, but only transmitted and transformed. A friend once remarked that 'the best gifts are given with a warm hand' (meaning while the giver is still alive). Your loving presence in life is your legacy, a source of light and energy that you can transmit in every conversation, every interaction, every gesture, and that will extend far beyond your physical continuance on earth.

This is the fullest fruit of your wisdom years, your finest and your lasting legacy to the future. The gift that will never stop giving.

PAUSE FOR THOUGHT

- Does the butterfly migration story help you to engage with these challenges in your own life?
- How do you feel about the parable of the new wineskins?
- How do these reflections connect to any situations in your own life?

- Which values matter most to you?
- How could you pass them on?
- How would you want to be remembered? How can you nourish, now, the qualities in yourself that you want to be remembered for?

EPILOGUE

All the flowers of all our tomorrows are in the seeds of today.
Indian proverb

HOW OFTEN DO we look at our children or grandchildren or those of our friends and wonder how it happened that these once tiny babies have become grown men and women, leading fruitful lives of their own?

Our physical lives, like theirs, also began their earth-adventure as tiny seeds and these seeds too have grown into trees big enough for birds to nest in, and we also wonder how that has happened.

The seeds of our inner lives, initially perhaps unnoticed and unacknowledged, have also been growing slowly and invisibly, making their soul journey through the years. They have been fed and watered by all our life experience, our reflections on it and our responses to it, gradually turning it into wisdom.

What began as a tiny seed has grown in stature and significance as we have grown in years. It has brought forth the green leaves and the blossom of our springtime and shed its autumn leaves as winter approaches. Just as the leaves of the forest capture sunlight and turn it into chemical energy to create the fuel of biological life, so our days have captured all our many and varied life experiences. We in turn have reflected on our experience and turned it into wisdom, the fuel of spiritual life.

Now our leaves are falling as we learn to let go of health and strength, status and energy. Our tree stands tall in the forest, its branches bare, its trunk gnarled and weather-beaten, a stark silhouette against the backdrop of the setting sun. It feels like the end of the story, but it is actually the beginning of a new chapter, because the blossom of springtime has been transformed into fruit. We have been growing our own unique wisdom tree. Each of our trees bears its

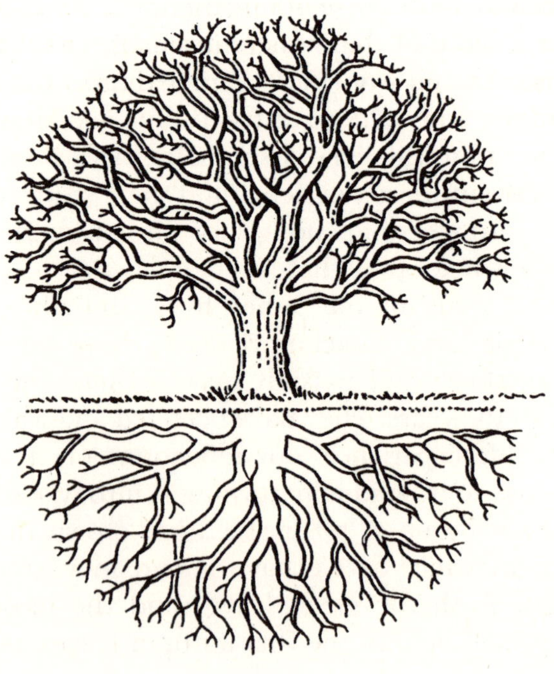

own kind of fruit just as the trees in the forest bear the berries and the beechnuts, the apples and the acorns.

We watch, perhaps dismayed, as our fruits fall to the ground in the storms of later life, storms that one way or another will soon cause our life's tree itself to fall. But Earth rejoices, because she understands that every fruit that falls and sinks into the ground carries the hidden promise of abundant new life to come. She knows that inside every acorn lies concealed not just another oak tree but potentially an entire forest of oak trees. The tiny seed that marked your own life's beginning has grown and ripened and now falls to the earth at your earthly life's ending to become more than you could possibly imagine,.

Friends and fellow forest-dwellers, let the forest be not a place of darkness and dread, but a place of promise. Let us stand tall, giving thanks for all our yesterdays, and then let us trustfully yield all we have become towards the creating of the flowers of all Earth's tomorrows.

ACKNOWLEDGEMENTS

THIS BOOK CAME about by accident. Several times I was asked to offer days of reflection on the subject of aging, and several times I refused, on the grounds that such an event would be better led by an 'older' person. Eventually the same request was issued by the Ignatian Spirituality Centre (ISC) in Glasgow, and this time I checked my birth certificate. My excuses had expired. So my sincere thanks go first to the Glasgow ISC, and to Catriona, Joan and John and all the team who together manage such a fine ship there and who also succeeded in ridding me of my illusion of still being 'too young'.

Since then I have explored this topic in various retreats and would like to mention especially the groups who shared, and contributed to these explorations in person, at The Coach House in Kilmuir in the Scottish Highlands, The Society of Mary and Martha at Sheldon in Devon and The Briery in Ilkley, Yorkshire. Thanks to Zoom these explorations have also been shared by The Companions in the Ministry of the Ignatian Spiritual Exercises and other friends in Australia and New Zealand facilitated from Adelaide, and retreatants at The Well spirituality centre in Chicago, USA. Thank you to all those who attended these events, bringing their own rich experience to the conversation, and to all those whose hospitality and organisation made them possible.

Not least, my very sincere thanks go to David Moloney and Helen Porter at Darton, Longman and Todd for your enthusiasm, encouragement and expertise, but above all for your enduring friendship and support through so many years.

ORIGINS OF THE STORIES USED IN THE BOOK

Stories are very important to me and I tend to gather them as a honeypot attracts bees. Story-telling is primarily an oral tradition, and most of the stories in the book are my own re-tellings inspired by stories I have come across during my travels, some of them originally published in two anthologies, *100 Wisdom Stories* and *100 More Wisdom Stories* (Lion Publishing). The original source of these stories is, for the most part, unknown, but the following list details their provenance as far as this is possible.

Chapter 1

The Golden Buddha	Re-telling of a traditional story
The Forever Tree	Margaret Silf

Chapter 2

The Monkey's Gift	Re-telling of a traditional African tale
The Human Qualities Contest	Margaret Silf
The Fisherman's Dream	Re-telling of a traditional story

Chapter 3

The man and the island	Re-telling of a Mediterranean story

Chapter 4

The bridge builder	Re-telling of a traditional story
The New Suit	Margaret Silf

Chapter 5

The platypus story	Re-telling of an Australian Aboriginal story
The quarrelling tools	Re-telling of a Swedish folk story
The three sisters	Re-telling of an Iroquois legend
The long-handled spoons	Re-telling of a traditional story

Chapter 6

The elusive mountain	Re-telling of a traditional story

Chapter 7

The two wolves	Re-telling of a Native American story
The bees and the trees	Re-telling of a traditional Sufi story
The puddlefish	Re-telling of a story re-told by Sharon Halsey-Hoover from *Along the Water's Edge* by David Juniper
What is a saint?	Re-telling of a traditional story

Chapter 8

The stream	Re-telling of a traditional story

Chapter 9

The angel's kiss	Re-telling of a traditional story
The chief's three sons	Re-telling of a traditional story
The truck driver's light	Margaret Silf